Growing Roses in Calgary

Calgary Rose Society
593 Silvergrove Drive NW
Calgary, Alberta, Canada T3B 4R9
403·288·7160

www.calgaryrosesociety.ca
info@calgaryrosesociety.ca

First Paperback Edition – July 2010
15 14 13 12 11 10 – 1 2 3 4 5 6 7 8 9 10

Library and Archives Canada Cataloguing in Publication

Growing Roses in Calgary / Calgary Rose Society. 1 st ed.

Includes index.
ISBN: 978-0-9811347-0-3

1. Rose culture—Alberta—Calgary. 2. Rose culture—Cold regions. 3. Roses—Effect of cold on.
I. Calgary Rose Society

SB411.5.C3G76 2010   635.9'3373409712338   c2009-900093-8

The book was made possible by the very generous support of the following:

Technical Credits:
Authors: Joan Altenhof, Terry Altenhof, Brian Rottenfusser and Lucy Weir.
Editor: Kyla Arden-Maki.
Photographs: The photographs were taken by Brian Rottenfusser and Terry Altenhof. Additional photographs were taken by Ev Altenhof, Susannah Anderson, Kyla Arden-Maki, Donna Balzer, Fred Bentler, Bob Crick, Joan Crick, Derrick Ditchburn, Jeremy Drought, Brent Johner, Richard Leung, Rob Longair, Cherie Lowe, Linda McGregor, Matthew Mitchell, Cheryl Moorehead, Karen Mychaluk, Joanne Nemeth, Shauneen O'Brien, Leon Popik, Lynette Schimming, Steve Scott, Dr. Joe Shorthouse, Abbi Singh, Jim Slobodian, Margaret Troy, Lucy Weir, Karin Wellington, Norm Wellington. Unless otherwise noted on page 144, all photographs were taken in gardens located in and around Calgary in the Chinook belt of Southern Alberta.
Illustrations: Julia Millen, Calgary, Alberta.
Interior, cover design and pre-press production: Jeremy Drought, *Last Impression Publishing Service*, Calgary, Alberta.
Proofreading: Kyla Arden-Maki and Brian Rottenfusser.
Indexing: Brian Rottenfusser
Front cover image: 'Gold Medal' taken by Terry Altenhof.

Printed in Canada by *Marquis Imprimeur Inc.*, Montmagny, Québec.

Growing Roses in Calgary

CALGARY

Rose

SOCIETY

CALGARY, ALBERTA, CANADA

Acknowledgements

A LARGE NUMBER OF MEMBERS AND FRIENDS of the *Calgary Rose Society* contributed to the content of this book by writing articles, submitting data on their favourite roses, opening their gardens to our photographers, editing individual sections or rose descriptions, providing encouragement, and being a sounding board through the long process of bringing this project to fruition.

In particular, Deb Francis sat in on much of the early editing, particularly on the classification of roses. Abbi Singh initially headed our fund raising efforts. Donna Balzer reviewed an early draft of the manuscript and made many constructive suggestions. Kyla Arden-Maki took the many words and sections, and edited them into a logical sequence that could be easily read.

Our thanks to Harrington Telford, VP of Marketing at *Greengate Garden Centres, Ltd.*, for access to garden tools, a photo studio and financial support underwriting the production of the book; Jeremy Drought, *Last Impression Publishing Service*, for his publishing consultation services, interior and cover design and pre-press production support; Julia Millen, for her delightful illustrations; and Connie Dye, Events & Publications Manager at the *Calgary Horticultural Society*, for providing us with the banner photo on p. 15 (from the garden of Cathy Schlosser) and the image of William Baffin on the trellis on p. 21 (from the garden of Connie Smith).

To attempt to list everyone who contributed is to risk missing someone, but we would like to thank them all, for without their contributions, the book would not have become what you now have in front of you.

We sincerely thank: Joe Aasland, Kyla Arden-Maki, Ron Ayotte, Donna Balzer, Pat Bengoechea, Joyce Bily, Claire Boulanger, Fred Bray, Sylvia Budd, Kathy Bugo, Richard Clayton, Phyllis Coulter, Bob Crick, Joan Crick, Elizabeth Dawson Grove, Barry Elve, Deb Francis, Susan Hamilton, Jenny Hart, Don Heimbecker (deceased), Anne Hokea, Jim Jackson, Naomi Johansen, Betty Kruhlak, Cherie Lowe, Jean Merkley, Linda McGregor, Bill McManus, Cheryl Mitchell, Matthew Mitchell, Karen Mychaluk, Cheryl Myers, Joanne Ogilvie, Dr. Terence and Edith Penelhum, Leon Popik, David Rottenfusser, Donna Rottenfusser, Michael Rottenfusser, Wanda Rottenfusser, Evelyn Salamanowicz, Don Sanders, Abbi Singh, Linda Trim, Margaret Troy, Marian T. Troy, Judy Trudeau, Petra van den Heuval, Ted Walsh, Karin Wellington, Norm Wellington, Catherine Williams and Mary Zorko.

Contents

Dedications

This book is dedicated to Phyllis Coulter, Fred Bray, the late Donald Heimbecker, and all of the former members of the Calgary Rose Society. They are the ones who showed that you really can grow beautiful roses in Calgary.

This book is also a tribute to the vision and commitment of Terry Altenhof. Terry passed away as Growing Roses in Calgary *was about to go to press, but he left his stamp on every page.*

Calgary Horticultural Society tour of the Altenhof garden, of which Terry was so proud, in July 2008.

I Introduction

GROWING ROSES IN CALGARY is rewarding. Many people mistakenly believe that Calgary's challenging growing conditions rule out the possibility of growing a wide variety of roses. We've written *Growing Roses in Calgary* to dispel this myth and to show that some of the most beautiful and prolific rose gardens can be found here. In fact, all of the photographs of roses in this book are from local gardens and should convince you that you can enjoy the beauty and fragrance of roses in your own backyard. We have one of the most active rose societies in Canada, proof that Calgary's unique climate does not deter people from successfully growing roses.

What makes Calgary rose gardens unique? Calgary's elevation of between 1,000 – 1,200 m (3,300 – 3,900 ft.) and location near the Foothills of the Rocky Mountains create a unique environment for growing roses. The cool summer nights enhance rose colour, extend the bloom period and diminish disease. Calgary's long, sunny summer days result in high growth rates for the roses. Calgary's rose growers also face some unique challenges. Calgary is located in Plant Hardiness Zone 3a which means that hardy roses will survive without winter protection but tender roses must be protected from cold winters, Chinook winds and late spring frosts. Our soil and municipal water supply have high alkalinity (pH = 7.7), but roses prefer slightly acidic soil. Other obstacles to overcome are the dense clay soils and lack of topsoil.

All of these unique growing conditions mean that reference books not specific to Calgary may give incorrect advice. The information presented in this book is based on many years' experience of producing beautiful roses in and around Calgary.

The information contained in this book is applicable to growing roses in the entire Chinook belt of southern Alberta, not just in Calgary. We've included some general background information on roses, including rose classification and landscaping with roses. Calgary specific information is found throughout, such as establishing and maintaining a rose garden, organic rose growing, winterizing roses in Calgary, lists of rose friends and foes, and a description of common rose diseases. Growing roses in containers, propagating roses and information on both the Calgary Rose Society and the Calgary Rose Show are all described.

We've compiled a list of 113 favourite hardy and tender roses that are all grown in Calgary by Calgary Rose Society members.

The book includes a glossary, a selected listing of additional reading material and a list of rose societies and organizations, as well as sources for purchasing roses online and in the Calgary area. Public rose gardens open for viewing during the summer around Alberta are also included.

We hope that this book will inspire you to grow a beautiful rose garden of your own.

2 History of the Calgary Rose Society

THE CALGARY ROSE SOCIETY WAS formed in 1960, in response to the increasing number of Calgarians who were growing roses. In the beginning, the Society had 14 members and the membership fee was only $1.00. Today, we have members from all over Alberta, from Pincher Creek to Edmonton.

The Society's main purposes are:

- to share and increase knowledge through regularly scheduled meetings and activities with other rosarians and horticulture experts;
- to educate and encourage people to grow and show roses in Calgary; and
- to assist other organizations in the use and care of roses for the beautification of Calgary.

A ROSEY NURSERY RHYME

Ring around the rozies,
A pocket full of posies,
Huista, huista!
All fall down!

We've all sung and danced to this nursery rhyme. But do you know what it means? This rhyme commemorates the Black Death, the plague that ravaged England and Europe in the 17th century. It was believed that the fragrance of flowers, especially roses, could protect or even cure a person suffering from bubonic plague that caused swellings in armpits and groins. However, if the plague affected your lungs, causing sneezing and coughing, and eventually pneumonia, then there was no cure. All fall down! Let's translate the rhyme into modern English:

Ring around the roses,
A pocket full of scented flowers,
Achoo, achoooo!
We're dead!

In 1969, the Society had its first rose competition in conjunction with the Calgary Horticultural Society's annual show and a small, independent rose show was also held. In 1974, in order to showcase the Queen of Flowers, the first annual rose show was held, with more than 500 entries. Rose shows have been held each year since that very successful event.

Over the years, the Society has organized trips to Missoula, Spokane, Vancouver and towns within Alberta to view rose gardens and meet other rosarians. The Calgary Rose Society also had the honour of hosting the New Zealand Rose Society in May 1971. The Society established a newsletter in 1968 and it was named the *Rose Round-Up* in 1972.

Since inception, the Calgary Rose Society has been active in our community. In the past, we have:

- planted and maintained rose beds in Confederation Park, at the Elbow Valley Senior Citizens Lodge, at Stampede Park in honour of Calgary's Centennial year and at the former Alberta Children's Hospital; and
- established a rose test garden in Glenmore Park.

At present, the Calgary Rose Society:

- holds general meetings six times per year with rosarian and horticultural guest speakers;
- publishes the *Rose Round-Up* newsletter six times per year;
- holds a miniature rose sale every Mother's Day weekend and at the Calgary Horticultural Society's annual spring garden show;
- holds an Annual Rose Show in late July or early August; and
- presents clinics that demonstrate spring cleanup of roses, planting, pruning, preparing roses for showing and winterizing roses.

Within Canada, there are more than 15 regional rose societies devoted to promoting roses and rose growing locally. The Canadian Rose Society is Canada's national rose organization that promotes the cultivation and enjoyment of roses throughout our country. Around the world, there are more than 40 national rose societies, including the Royal National Rose Society in the United Kingdom and the American Rose Society in the United States.

3 *Classification of Roses*

KNOWLEDGE OF THE MAJOR CATEGORIES of roses will help in choosing roses for your garden and in growing them successfully. In the 18th century, Carolus Linnaeus and his followers began the complicated job of categorizing and naming roses. They created the genus Rosa that was then subdivided into several family groups. The main rose groups included herein are based on Linnaeus' work, although they have been expanded as new types of roses have been developed or discovered.

In North America, roses are classified according to standards published by the American Rose Society, which differ slightly from that of the rest of the world. There are four main groups: Species roses, Old Garden roses, Repeat Flowering Old Garden roses and Modern roses.

Rose Classification

Species Roses

A Species rose refers to a wild or native rose, all of which originated in the Northern Hemisphere. There are over 150 named Species roses throughout the world. Both the Canadian and the American Rose Societies include many Species as top rated roses.

Species rose blooms are usually single or, rarely, semi-double or double in shades of white, pink, red and yellow. Most Species are very fragrant. They bloom once a year in late spring or early summer over a period of 3 to 4 weeks, a short but outstanding display. Some bloom only on old wood, others bloom only on new wood.

Species roses have few requirements and are relatively disease free. They should be planted in a sunny location allowing enough room for the size of the mature plant. Once established, Species roses can tolerate less sun and water than other roses. It is not necessary to remove spent blooms as these roses only bloom once. The mature hips provide autumn and winter interest in the garden as well as food for the birds. Fertilizing is not required, but a feeding once a season will benefit the roses.

Suckering can be a problem with Species roses. Selected suckers at the base of the crown can be removed to control spreading. Alternatively, use a barrier around the rose to limit its size or choose plants that are grafted onto rootstock, although this can decrease the plant hardiness. Species roses can easily be propagated from suckers or root cuttings.

Species roses vary in hardiness depending on their geographical origin; the hardiness will be recorded on the label when the rose is purchased. Winter protection is not required for the hardy Species but for less hardy Species, a covering of

mulch is advised. For newly planted Species roses, a mulch covering is recommended for the first few winters until the plant is established. When a bush is about 5 years old, removing one or two older, thicker canes will help maintain vigour and stimulate the development of basal shoots.

When Species roses are mentioned, people tend to think first of the native prairie roses. Some of the Species roses native to Alberta are *R. acicularis* (also known as the 'Prickly Rose', the Alberta floral emblem), *R. arkansana* (the 'Prairie Rose') and *R. woodsii* (the 'Common Wild Rose'). These roses can be seen growing along roadsides and in parklands. However, these roses have not been extensively used in the garden setting due to their short blooming period and tendency to sucker.

Many gardeners may be unknowingly growing a Species rose, perhaps the beautiful *R. foetida* 'bicolour' ('Austrian Copper'), *R. foetida* 'persiana' ('Persian Yellow') or *R. rubrifolia* ('Red Leaf Rose'). Other less common but excellent Species roses that are hardy in Calgary include: *R. blanda, R. carolina, R. eglanteria, R. forrestiana, R. hugonis, R. laxa, R. nutkana, R. pendulina, R. pomifera, R. primula* and *R. rugosa*.

Old Garden Roses

Old Garden roses (OGR) include all roses developed before the advent of the Hybrid Teas in 1867. This is a large and diverse group comprising many classes and their cultivars. The oldest roses in this group, established before the end of the 18th century, include the Gallicas, Damasks, Albas, Centifolias and Mosses. All Old Garden roses are tender and require winter protection in Calgary.

Gallica Roses

Gallicas are the oldest of the Old Garden roses and are believed to be the ancestors of many other classes. They were cultivated by the Persians as early as the 12th century B.C. At one time there were more than 900 named cultivars but there are only about 50 cultivars available today. This group grows well in Calgary and is tolerant of poor soil.

Gallicas have a dense upright growth habit and range in size from 0.9 to 1.5 m (3 to 5 ft.) in height and width. The Gallica colour range includes pinks, rich crimson, purples and red blends and a few are

Austrian Copper

Rosa Mundi

Madame Hardy

striped. The blossoms can be single, semi-double or very double. They are heavy one-time bloomers and most are very fragrant. The foliage is somewhat coarse and dark green with a few small prickles on the stems.

Allow plenty of room for growth and root development as these shrubs develop by suckering. While tolerant of poor soil, these roses will perform best when well watered and fed. These shrubs bloom on previous year's wood, so do not prune until after they finish blooming and only prune to shape. Winter protection of the whole plant is important as Gallicas bloom at the ends of the canes.

Examples of Gallica roses that grow well in Calgary are: 'Empress Josephine', 'Rosa Mundi', 'Apothecary's Rose' and 'Alain Blanchard'.

Damask Roses

Damasks are younger than the Gallicas. The Persians were again the first to cultivate the Damask rose.

Damasks are usually one-time bloomers with an extremely strong fragrance. They will grow to 1.5 m (5 ft.) in height in the Calgary area. The canes, thicker than those of the Gallicas, tend to arch and are covered in both large and small hooked prickles. The leaves are soft, hairy and medium green. The blossoms can be semi-double to very double and range from white and light pink to medium pink.

These roses perform best with adequate water and fertilizing. Damask roses typically bloom on old wood, so prune after the bloom season is finished. Good winter protection is required to survive Calgary winters.

Examples of Damask roses are 'Madame Hardy', 'Ispahan' and 'La Ville de Bruxelles'. 'Quatre Saisons' may repeat bloom at the end of summer.

Alba Roses

Albas have been in existence since medieval times. They are believed to have originated from a naturally occurring cross of a Damask rose and the Species *R. canina*.

These tall, shrubby plants can sometimes reach 1.8 m (6 ft.) in height and are covered with pale blue-green disease-resistant foliage. Flowers are produced along the length of the canes, especially if the canes are arching. The very double blooms are extremely fragrant and are mostly white, off-white or pale pink in colour. The scarlet hips are long and smooth.

The Albas will tolerate shade but will bloom better with full sun. They are generally undemanding plants. Like the Damasks, prune Albas after flowering, if needed. The removal of old canes will stimulate the development of basal shoots. Albas typically grow quickly and are fairly hardy but still require some winter protection to preserve the flowering canes.

'Madame Plantier', 'Félicité Parmentier', 'Königin von Dänemark' and 'Maiden's Blush' ('Cuisse de Nymphe') are to be found growing happily in Calgary.

Félicité Parmentier

OLD GARDEN ROSE GROWTH IN CALGARY

- Most reference books listing Old Garden roses describe shrub heights taller than are typically achieved in Calgary's short summers. Therefore, only a light pruning of Old Garden roses is necessary here, much less than usually recommended.
- Many taller growing shrubs can be pegged or trained horizontally to maximize the development of flower-bearing laterals.
- A sheltered location is preferred to decrease winter die back.
- Good winter protection is required to preserve the canes.

Centifolia Roses

Centifolias originated in the 17th Century in Holland and are sometimes referred to as the Cabbage roses. These one-time bloomers were extensively painted by 17th and 18th century Dutch artists.

Centifolias range in height from 1 to 2.1 m (3 to 7 ft.) and are lax and sprawling in habit. They are extremely fragrant with huge, very double blooms in colours ranging from pink, mauve and purple to red. The petal count is anywhere from 60 – 100 petals per bloom. These roses rarely set seed.

Centifolias can be prone to powdery mildew. They bloom only on the previous year's growth, so prune only after flowering, to shape or to remove dead wood. These roses are not crown-hardy, which means in severe winters they may die back to the ground. While the plant will grow again, no blooms will be produced that year. Good winter protection is essential to preserve the flower producing canes.

'Robert le Diable', 'Fantin-Latour' and 'Tour de Malakoff' grow well here.

Fantin-Latour

Moss Roses

The first Moss rose (*Rosa centifolia muscosa*) was discovered in the late seventeenth century and was a sport or mutation of a Centifolia rose. Since then, hundreds of varieties have been bred.

Moss roses may have a moss-like growth, also known as whiskers, on their stems, calyxes

Salet

and/or sepals. The semi-double to very double blossoms range in colours from white, pink, mauve, purple to maroon, and are extremely fragrant but, unfortunately, sterile. Moss roses range in size from miniatures to huge shrubs and bloom once a summer.

As with the other Old Garden roses, winter protection is required for Moss roses to survive Calgary winters. Prune Mosses in the summer after flowering to remove dead wood or to shape the plant.

'Henri Martin', 'Salet', 'William Lobb', 'Chapeau de Napoléon', 'Dresden Doll' and 'Deuil de Paul Fontaine' are found in many Calgary gardens.

Repeat Flowering Old Garden Roses

At the end of the 18th century, a repeat blooming rose from China was introduced to Europe, changing the history of roses forever. Hybridizers began crossing this repeat bloomer with the once blooming, larger roses of Europe and the Middle East to yield repeat blooming, large flowered roses.

Empress Josephine Bonaparte was passionate about roses and acquired a massive collection of them. In 1799, she purchased Malmaison, a château located in France on 650 acres, for her roses. She hired the greatest botanists of her day and, with her encouragement, French rose breeding expanded rapidly. The happy coincidence of the introduction of the repeat flowering roses from China and the enthusiasm fueled by Empress Josephine led to great experimentation and the development of whole new classes of roses.

China Roses

China roses will grow to 60 cm (2 ft.) in height and bloom intermittently. However, they are generally not grown in Calgary as they prefer a milder climate. They will not survive Calgary's winters, even with protection. Any rose with a China parent may also have trouble surviving Calgary's climate.

Noisette Roses

The first Noisette rose, 'Champneys' Pink Cluster', was the result of a cross between *Rosa moschata* and the China rose 'Parsons' Pink' by a rose breeder (John Champney) from the southern USA in 1802.

Noisette roses are cluster-flowered, recurrent, tall growing and climbing or bushy in habit.

The Canadian winter is far too harsh for Noisettes as they tend to keep growing later in the season, making them susceptible to damage.

Portland Roses

The first Portland rose was discovered in the early 1800s in Italy. It was likely the result of a cross between a China rose and the Damask 'Autumn Rose'. The rose, and the family, were named after the Duchess of Portland, who introduced it to England. By 1850, the Portlands were so popular that the French had bred over 150 varieties.

This is a beautiful class of roses that reach 1 m (3 ft.) in height. The blooms are relatively small, very double, fragrant and produced on very short stems. Colours range from deep pinks and purples to reds. These roses bloom well and can repeat.

Indigo

Portland roses should only be pruned to remove dead wood. As they are descended from China roses, good winter protection is required to survive Calgary winters.

Portlands grown successfully in Calgary include: 'Indigo', 'Jacques Cartier' ('Marchesa Boccella'), 'Rose de Rescht' and 'Comte de Chambord'.

Bourbon Roses

Bourbon roses were discovered in the early 19th century on the Ile de Bourbon, a small island in the Indian Ocean. Homes on the island were surrounded by hedges consisting of a mixture of China and Damask roses which produced a natural cross. This cross was then refined by the hybridizers to create the Bourbon roses.

Bourbons are tall shrubs reaching 1.2 m (4 ft.) in Calgary. Their blooms are white, pink or red in colour. Bourbons are renowned for extremely fragrant blooms. They repeat well.

As with the Portland roses, Bourbon roses should be pruned only to shape or to remove dead wood. They must be well protected to survive the winters in Calgary.

'Madame Doré,' 'Reine de Victoria' and 'Louise Odier' are three Bourbons that are currently being grown in Calgary.

Madame Doré

Hybrid Perpetual Roses

Hybrid Perpetuals were developed in the 19th century in response to immense public demand for repeat blooming roses for both the garden and floral arrangements. Over 3000 new cultivars were introduced as Hybrid Perpetuals during the Victorian Era but regrettably not all of the roses were of good quality. Unfortunately, the majority of hybridization records for the Hybrid Perpetuals have been lost, so the parentage of many is unclear. Hybrid Perpetuals are a transition between the Old Garden roses and the Hybrid Teas.

Shrub size varies greatly, but most have large, fully double, very fragrant blooms that are long lasting. Colours range from white and pink to dark crimson. All require good winter protection.

Named varieties that grow well in this area include: 'Mrs. John Laing', 'Ferdinand Pichard', 'Baronne Prévost', 'Enfant de France', 'Empereur du Maroc', 'Baroness Rothschild', 'Paul Neyron' and 'Reine des Violettes'.

Baroness Rothschild

Tea Roses

Tea roses were derived by crossing Bourbon or Noisette roses with China roses. The first Tea Rose was introduced to England in 1808. The blooms of these roses smell like fresh tea leaves. They were initially called Tea Scented China roses, which was eventually shortened to Tea roses.

Teas consist of rather spindly bushes with high centered blooms that resemble the Hybrid Teas of today. Colours range from yellow, apricot, white and pink to dark red. These roses require long summers to flourish. Also, these roses are very tender, making them unsuitable for Calgary's climate.

Modern Roses

Modern roses are defined as those roses that have appeared since the introduction of the Hybrid Tea 'La France' by the French breeder, Jean-Baptiste Guillot, in 1867.

The Modern roses category includes the Hybrid Teas, Polyanthas, Floribundas, Grandifloras, Miniatures, Modern Shrubs and English roses. With very few exceptions, these are all repeat bloomers and require deadheading to promote blooming.

Hybrid Teas

Today, Hybrid Teas are the most popular class of roses. They have a wide range of colours, hardiness and disease resistance. Breeding of Hybrid Teas was begun as early as 1815 by crossing Hybrid Perpetuals and Tea roses.

Typically Hybrid Teas are upright shrubs and usually the flowers are produced singly or in small clusters on long, sturdy stems. They are excellent for cutting or displaying at rose shows. All cultivars are tender and require winter protection. Roses usually sold by florists are very tender Hybrid Teas.

Big Purple

Polyanthas

In 1865, a low-growing, non-recurrent form of *Rosa multiflora* was brought to England from China and was soon widely distributed in Europe. Polyanthas resulted from crossing this dwarf *R. multiflora* with dwarf China roses. Unfortunately, few Polyanthas are available today, having been displaced by the more popular Floribundas.

The Fairy

Polyanthas are short, floriferous bushes covered in trusses of small, scentless, single or double blooms. They are good ground cover or border roses due to their low-growing habit and profusion of blooms. Winter protection is required.

'The Fairy' is widely grown in Calgary and is a strong performer.

Floribundas

In 1909, Hybrid Teas were crossed with Polyanthas in an effort to develop hardier roses that would bloom in short summers. The resulting roses were named Floribundas.

Floribundas are strong, vigorous growers, usually shorter than Hybrid Teas. They produce clusters of smaller flowers in a variety of colours including bicolours. Many have a light to moderate fragrance. Floribundas are hardier than Hybrid Teas but still require winter protection in the Calgary area.

Honey Perfume

Grandifloras

The first Grandiflora, 'Queen Elizabeth', was the result of a cross between the Hybrid Tea 'Charlotte Armstrong' and the Floribunda 'Flora Dora'. It showed exceptionally strong growth with large blooms produced in clusters. The American Rose Society deemed it sufficiently different from both Hybrid Teas and Floribundas to create a new class, the Grandifloras, in 1954. In Europe, Grandiflora roses are considered to be Hybrid Teas.

Grandiflora bushes are generally taller than those of most Hybrid Teas with slightly smaller blooms. The stems are long like a Hybrid Tea and the flowers are produced in clusters. Winter protection of Grandiflora roses is required in Calgary.

Queen Elizabeth

Miniatures

In the early 1800s, Robert Sweet discovered a dwarf rose growing in the botanical gardens in Mauritius and brought the rose to England. Miniature roses enjoyed a brief period of popularity and then virtually disappeared. They were rediscovered in pots on windowsills in a small village in Switzerland in 1917. Hybridizers became interested and began work with Miniature roses in Holland and Spain.

By 1935, Miniature roses had been introduced into the United States, where Ralph Moore of California acquired plants from those early hybridizers, and began his own breeding program. The overwhelming success of miniature roses is credited to Mr. Moore who began to cross existing Miniatures with almost every known rose type, leading to an explosion in the number of varieties available.

Miniature roses fit easily into the landscape in either beds or containers, bloom repeatedly and are fairly winter hardy as they are grown on their own roots. Adequate winter protection for Minis grown in containers is easily achieved by moving the pots

Raspberry Punch

to a frost-free environment or planting the rose in the ground and covering with mulch, peat moss or leaves.

Modern Shrubs

These roses are cultivars, complex hybrids of species roses and modern roses, not Species roses. Modern Shrubs can be hardy or tender depending on their parentage and are a wonderful addition to the landscape.

There are several series of Modern Shrubs developed by the Rose Development Program of Agriculture Canada to produce a wide choice of roses suitable for our climate. These series include the Explorer roses, named for famous Canadian explorers, the Morden Parkland roses and the more recent Canadian Artist series. The Pavement series, developed in Germany, is another notable group of hardy shrubs. Many other hardy shrubs, including some bred by Canadian hybridizers, will perform well in Calgary.

Hardy shrubs do not need winter protection, but most will benefit from a crown mulch for the first winter or two until established. Young canes or cane tips may suffer winterkill due to the freeze/thaw cycles of Calgary winters and wind desiccation. The roses should not be fertilized with nitrogen after August 15; this will reduce the growth of new canes that are most susceptible to winter damage.

It may be awkward to overwinter tender Modern Shrubs due to their large size. The shrubs can be pruned to a manageable size for covering but then the full blooming potential and natural grace of the shrub will be lost. Alternatively, canes can be bent down and covered with mulch. Fortunately, if the canes suffer winterkill, the bush itself will likely survive.

Excellent hardy shrub performers in Calgary are: any Spinosissima, most Hybrid Rugosas, 'John Davis', 'John Cabot', 'Thérèse Bugnet', 'Persian Yellow', 'Wasagaming' and 'Hope for Humanity'.

English or Austin Roses

In 1960, David Austin, an English hybridizer, started crossing Old Garden roses with Hybrid Teas. 'Constance Spry' was the first successful cross, released in 1961. Since then, well over a hundred beautiful English or Austin roses have been introduced. In 1969, Austin introduced his first repeat blooming roses, a series named after the characters in Chaucer's Canterbury Tales.

English roses have large, cupped blossoms, resembling Old Garden roses. They generally have a strong fragrance and many are vigorous growers. Some plants have weak necks that allow the flowers to droop. Consistent watering with a weeper hose will help the canes maintain turgor and stay erect.

Many English roses are somewhat hardier than Hybrid Teas but all require winter protection.

A few English roses that perform well in Calgary are: 'Mary Rose', 'Evelyn', 'Abraham Darby', 'Heritage', 'Graham Thomas' and 'Winchester Cathedral'.

Abraham Darby

ROSES THROUGH TIME

Roses are one of the most popular flowering plants in the world and there are thousands of different roses grown today. Roses were cultivated in China over five thousand years ago. The oldest known roses are fossils from the United States and China, dating to 32 million years before present.

Hope for Humanity

MINIATURE ROSES

Miniature roses are so prevalent these days that it's worth devoting some special attention to them. They are perfect plants for a number of locations, such as bed or border edgings, accent plants in rock gardens, garden containers or even as houseplants. There is a huge choice in the colours, fragrances and sizes available, but all are semi-hardy, continuous bloomers. And their smaller size means you can fit more into your garden!

There are six different groups of small garden roses:

Micro Miniature

Micro-minis typically grow 15 to 30 cm (6–12 in.) in height with blossoms 0.5 to 2 cm ($\frac{1}{4}$–1 in.) across. Only a few cultivars of this type are available, such as 'Sweet Fairy' with fragrant, pale pink blossoms and 'Cinderella' with white, pompom shaped blossoms.

Cinderella

Mini Roses

These roses generally grow 30–45 cm (12–18 in.) in height with foliage and blooms in proportion. A popular mini grown in Calgary is 'Rainbow's End' with bright yellow blooms flushed with red which intensifies in bright sunlight. Another, 'Lavender Crystal', has fragrant lavender blooms.

Lavender Crystal

Mini Climbers

Mini climbers produce long canes which can be trained to grow on supports. 'Jeanne Lajoie' will grow to a height of 1.2 m (4 ft.) and produce soft pink blooms in flushes all summer. 'Warm Welcome', a fragrant orange, has very thorny canes that stretch to 1.2 m (4 ft.) in height.

Warm Welcome

Trailers

These plants have a cascading growth habit perfect for baskets and over walls. 'Sweet Chariot' produces bunches of very fragrant lavender blend blooms from mid-summer until frost. 'Green Ice' is a hardy plant with unusual blooms that start out as pinkish buds, open to double, white flowers and age to a cool light green.

Green Ice

Mini Flora or Patio

Patio roses have a slightly larger plant and bloom size than most miniature roses. Average plant size is 45–75 cm (1.5–2.5 ft.). 'Ingrid' has red and yellow flowers and 'Flower Power' produces prolific flushes of apricot orange blooms.

Flower Power

Mini Moss

Moss roses have fine soft hairs on the buds and stems. 'Dresden Doll' has soft pink blooms. 'Fuzzy Wuzzy Red' has clusters of bright red blooms and the mossy buds are fragrant when touched. Both grow to about 30 cm (12 in.) in height.

Fuzzy Wuzzy Red

Miniature roses can be purchased at local garden centres or from online rose nurseries. The biggest supplier of Miniature roses in southern Alberta is the Calgary Rose Society. The Society holds two sales each spring, one in conjunction with the Calgary Horticultural Society's spring garden show and the other on the Mother's Day weekend; check the society's website for more details <**www.calgaryrosesociety.ca**>.

Miniature roses should be treated as full sized roses for planting, fertilizing, watering and pruning, as described in chapters 5 and 6, *Establishing a Rose Garden* and *Maintaining a Rose Garden*. Miniature roses are generally grown on their own roots, so while winter protection is recommended, a lot may not be required; see chapter 7, *Winterizing Roses*, for further details.

Miniature Roses as House Plants

Miniature roses can survive and bloom inside your house, adding a touch of colour during the coldest part of the winter. They are however, outdoor plants at heart, so a little effort is required to keep them looking and doing their best.

Mini roses for the house can be purchased at garden centres in the fall and winter. If the rose pot is quite small, you will need to repot the rose. You can also bring a favourite Mini from the garden into the house, before fall freeze-up. Minis taken from the garden should be cut short, defoliated, sprayed with insecticidal soap to reduce the pests that might catch a ride inside and repotted. The container for the rose should be at least 15 – 20 cm (6 – 8") in diameter to support adequate growth.

Like all roses, Miniature rose houseplants need full sun and adequate humidity. The optimal location for your indoor Minis is in a south-facing window or under grow lights, away from vents and radiators. As the indoor humidity drops during the winter months, the roses can quickly become desiccated. Watch the leaves carefully, if they start to turn yellow and brown, you can increase the humidity by setting the container on pebbles in a tray of water.

Too much heat or water or too little light puts stress on the rose, making it prone to aphids, spider mites, powdery mildew and black spot, even indoors. Give the roses a weekly shower to reduce the attacks of these pests. Thoroughly rinse both the tops and the undersides of the leaves. If pests persist, spray with insecticidal soap.

After Miniature roses spend a season indoors, put them outdoors for the summer to recover. They can be planted directly in the garden or kept in containers, but they should be repotted into larger containers that will not dry out quickly. Don't forget to harden the roses off before leaving them outdoors permanently. Make sure they receive plenty of sun, rich soil and water, and mulch them well when next winter comes. With proper care, they will live happily for many years, indoors or outside.

Parade Series Red

Landscaping with Roses

ROSES LEND THEMSELVES TO A VARIETY of applications in the landscape, whether as a garden focus or as a complement to existing plants. Roses can be used as hedges, ground covers, borders, companion plants to perennials and even in pots on a deck or patio. They can be trained on garden structures or used to camouflage unsightly areas. Their uses are limited only by the imagination.

Although the details of hard landscaping are beyond the scope of this book, we have included a few ideas for designing a brand new rose garden and for enhancing an existing garden by planting roses. After all, if roses are your passion, then they should be predominant in your garden.

Roses in the Garden

Before you start digging beds for roses or rearranging existing plants, you need to evaluate how you want your garden to function. You need to have an idea of what you want the end product to be before any work is done. Careful planning and consideration of elements will result in a visually pleasing design with ease of maintenance.

When designing your beds, consider the mature size of the plants, as shrubs vary greatly in form, height and width. Some sprawling shrubs require a generous space for proper display, maintenance and air circulation. Species roses and some own-root shrubs tend to sucker and may need to be placed where there is ample room to spread. Keep thorny roses away from walkways. Create paths for access through the beds to avoid compaction of the soil. Allow a generous area around tender roses and climbers, as they need to be removed from supports and covered for the winter.

You need to consider the future use of the yard space as access paths and entertainment areas must be located before positioning any rose beds. Entertainment spaces such as decks and patios

are excellent areas to display roses and enjoy their fragrance. Children and pets need areas of grass for playing; rose plantings and play areas should be separated for the safety of both the children and the roses. Barriers may be needed around rose beds to keep pets out.

Garden Styles

You need to choose a style for your garden that fits with the surrounding landscape, works with the size and type of buildings and reflects your personal taste. Different garden styles evoke different feelings and impressions for visitors.

There are three basic garden styles to consider in creating your desired look and effect: formal, semi-formal and informal. Variations of either a single garden style or a combination of styles can be adapted to any yard. Your garden is your haven and should reflect your personality and taste.

The Formal Garden

The keys to the formal garden are geometry, symmetry and repetition of colour, form and design. Formal beds are usually situated in the centre of the landscape or near a building to enhance a formal or grand home.

In a formal garden, a central structure such as statuary or a fountain anchors the framework. Beds and paths are arranged as mirror images along an axis.

Strong lines, straight paths, central structural features and repeating geometric patterns give the impression of strength, stability, order and control. Roses are displayed in mass plantings, each bed a single variety. Lawns are manicured and the beds are edged in low growing clipped shrubs. Boxwood is commonly used in milder climates but in Calgary, herbs, annuals or leafy perennials can be used, providing they can be clipped.

A formal style garden is commonly found in the gardens of European estates, grand homes and public gardens. The focus of the formal garden is the design rather than the plantings. A large area is required for a formal garden.

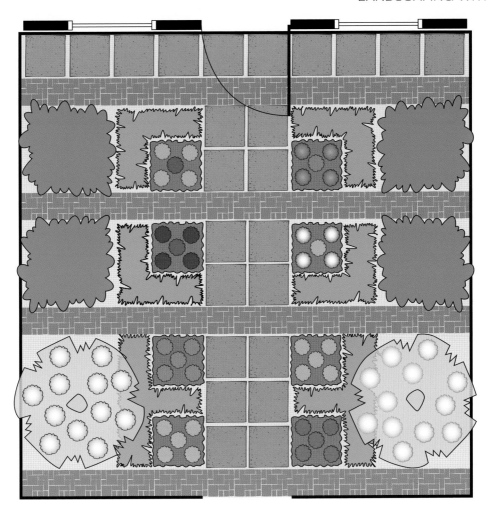

The formal garden

The Semiformal Garden

The semiformal garden incorporates some elements of geometry but in a much more relaxed fashion. The key to this design is balance instead of strict symmetry.

Island beds may be free form in shape with curved perimeter beds. There are more mixed plantings and less clipping and sculpting of shrubs than in the formal garden. Statuary enhances plantings rather than being the main focus. The lawn plays an important part in connecting parts of the garden. Curved borders lead the viewer through the garden in a leisurely manner and soften the geometric lines of buildings.

Balance and repetition still influence the placement of plants but in a less rigid manner. The plant is the focus of the semiformal garden.

The Informal Garden

The key to this style of garden is playful, easy-going and simple rather than complex. Plantings are arranged to create venues.

The cues for an informal garden are taken from existing trees, shrubs and contours. This is perhaps the most difficult style in which to achieve pleasing results as plants must be selected and placed carefully to avoid a chaotic appearance. Edges are blurred between woodland and garden, beds are curved and overflowing. Paths meander, and ornaments and sculptures are used as a surprise rather than as a focus. Any roses are part of companion plantings and are left to ramble and lean.

The focus of an informal garden is the incorporation of the garden into a natural setting. English country, casual and woodland gardens are all examples of informal garden styles.

Design Principles

Three basic design principles apply to landscaping: balance, proportion and repetition. Additionally, the use of colour, texture and form in plant material and garden structures can result in a harmonious and unified garden design.

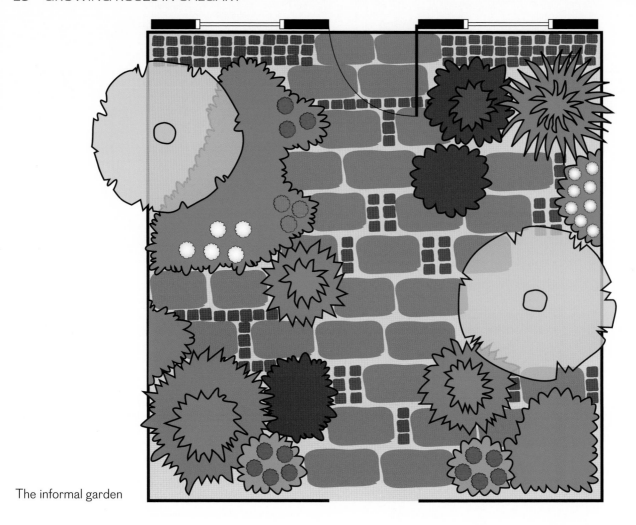

The informal garden

Balance

Balance within the garden depends on the basic garden style employed. Formal gardens are well balanced as the plantings are symmetrical and mirror images. The semiformal garden has less rigid adherence to symmetry but balance is still maintained. The informal garden has an overall sense of balance with groupings of plants or shrubs that have a variety of shapes and sizes.

Proportion

Flowerbeds, trees and shrubs in the garden should be in proportion to the buildings, structures and size of the yard. Small yards and houses require smaller trees. Manmade structures should not dominate at the expense of the flower display. Adequate space should be allowed for mature plants.

Repetition

A sense of unity and rhythm can be created by repeating sizes, leaf shapes, colours and shrub forms throughout the garden. Colour is a matter of personal taste and is used to create a mood or response; soft colours calm the viewer whereas bright colours excite. Consideration should be given to choosing flowers that will complement the colour of the home and any fences. Fall colour in foliage, berries and hips will extend the seasonal display.

Contrasting textures in foliage and blooms add visual interest and relief. For example, broad leaves enhance the effect of feathery ones. Foliage patterns can be enhanced by adding garden ornamentation such as statuary, glass globes and stone.

Plant shape or form also plays an important role in creating interest. Shape variations and focal points, such as groupings of rounded, tall, spiky or creeping forms, keep the eye travelling and intrigued. Vertical, central or horizontal elements repeated throughout the garden create rhythm and unity to the plantings and contribute to a sense of balance. For example, a climbing rose may be trained on an obelisk, surrounded by Hybrid Teas or small shrub roses, with creeping roses planted at the base. Alternatively, allow a clematis to climb a trellis, plant Floribundas at the base and edge with creeping thyme.

Roses for Special Uses

Roses can be used for a number of different things within a garden: as a focus, as an enhancement to a perennial garden, or as a shield for a structure. The purpose of the planting will control the choice of rose.

Hedges
Hedges define property borders, separate areas of the garden, enhance structures, provide privacy and security or redirect foot traffic. The best rose for a hedge is a shrub that tolerates pruning, retains foliage to the base of the plant, requires little maintenance and is disease resistant.

Winter coverage of a hedge is not practical, so choose hardy varieties. Suckering can be a problem or an advantage, depending on the size of hedge desired; allow suckers to survive if a larger hedge is needed. Hardy rugosa hybrids make excellent large hedges whereas species roses make good natural hedges in woodland settings. *Rosa rubrifolia* forms a beautiful, easily pruned hedge with its bluish cast, extreme hardiness and disease resistance.

Islands
Islands of blooming roses draw the eye and highlight that portion of the garden. Edging an island with low growing annuals or herbs imparts a more formal look to the garden and camouflages any bare shrub bases. Planted edging also softens the look of the stiff growth habit of Hybrid Tea roses. Within an island, a centre piece such as a bird bath, obelisk, statue or water fountain creates a focal point.

A mass planting of one cultivar makes a bold statement and shows the rose to best advantage.

A mix of cultivars is also attractive, but requires planning to create a complementary colour scheme and to balance different plant sizes. In mixed plantings, groupings of 3 to 5 plants of one cultivar look best.

Cutting Gardens
To provide cut flowers for arrangements, a mix of colours within the rose garden is recommended. Any clashing bloom colours can be subdued by adding perennials, annuals or herbs in white, blues and greens. The best roses for cutting are Hybrid Teas, Floribundas and Grandifloras. Beautiful, fragrant arrangements can be made with English and Old Garden roses.

Ground Covers
Ground covers are useful in creating visual connections between plantings as well as covering bare areas and the base of shrubs. They can be used to link plantings to hard structures such as rocks or brick walls and are perfect in small spaces or on slopes.

Some trailing ground cover roses, such as 'Max Graf' and *R. spinosissima*, will cover a large area at maturity. Others, such as 'Nozomi', are smaller and more suitable for confined spaces.

Visual Backdrop

Many roses, such as *R. rubrifolia*, have cool blue-green foliage that can enhance surrounding plants. Interspersing ferny roses, such as the Spinosissimas, between Hybrid Teas or Floribundas will add interest to a garden and break the monotony of homogeneous plantings.

Once-blooming shrubs, such as the species roses, the Spinosissimas and most Old Garden roses, provide early summer colour. Once they have finished blooming, the mass of green foliage provides a restful backdrop to the first major flush of the Hybrid Teas.

Guerrilla Gardening

The beautification of alleys and otherwise neglected spaces can be achieved through the use of low maintenance rose shrubs. Species roses are particularly well suited to these areas as they can thrive in poor soil without added fertilizers and watering. These roses can be planted with perennials with similar needs.

R. forrestiana in an alley

Roses on Structures

Climbing roses are those that produce long arching canes. However, roses are not true climbing plants; the canes need to be trained or attached to supports in order to climb on structures. Almost any structure within a garden can be used to support a climbing rose.

Climbers supported on fences create a vertical accent at the back of the garden. Climbers supported on trellises or pillars provide vertical focuses within rose plantings. Climbing roses also can be trained to grow horizontally by bending and tying canes to horizontal structures. This will also stimulate the growth of flower-producing laterals.

The nature and amount of each rose's growth should be considered before planting it against any structure. A rose whose base is very wide at maturity will quickly outgrow a small structure if it produces suckers. On the other hand, many tender climbers are so stiff that they cannot be bent to the ground for winter protection but must be pruned, reducing the size they can attain the following year.

Walls and Fences

If you are trying to cover a tall structure, a few Species and hardy Explorer roses are capable of reaching heights of 3 m (10 ft.). These are also recommended for more exposed locations as they will not require winter protection in Calgary. Some less hardy climbers can be grown against houses or heated garages if the location is protected from the wind and there is a warmer microclimate. However, roses grown under eaves will suffer from dry soil conditions and will need increased watering. Many climbing roses, such as ramblers, will not survive Calgary winters, making it difficult for them to grow tall enough to cover even protected walls or fences. If you choose to use a less hardy rose to

John Davis

ROSE FACTS & TRIVIA

- Rose—the name is derived from the Latin *rosa* and the Greek *rhodon*.
- Depictions of roses were used to decorate jewellery, vases and utensils of the long extinct Minoan civilization on the Aegean island of Crete.
- Roses are depicted on walls of Egyptian tombs dating from approximately 700 BC to the time of Roman influence.
- Roses are recognized as symbols of youth, beauty, desire and love.
- The shield of Achilles was decorated with roses.
- According to the Iliad, the goddess Aphrodite used oil of roses to anoint the body of the slain Hector.
- Aphrodite presented a rose to her son Eros, who in turn gave it to the god of silence, Harpocrates. Therefore, the rose was recognized as a symbol of discretion. In some council chambers in medieval Europe, a rose was suspended from the ceiling to remind councillors to keep the proceedings confidential. The meeting was said to have been conducted "under the rose" or "sub rosa".
- In Greek mythology, all roses were originally white. Some changed to red when they were spattered with the blood of Venus.
- The ancient Romans cultivated roses in greenhouses heated by hot water plumbing. Rose oil was used as perfume. Rose petals were scattered in public squares at festivals, triumphs, gladiatorial contests and on guests at orgies.
- According to Confucius (~551 to 479 BC), roses were cultivated and admired in the gardens of the imperial Chu dynasty.

climb a structure, consider using a companion vine, such as a clematis, that will increase the height covered.

Obelisks, Tuteurs, Pillars, Trellises and Pergolas
It is important to choose hardy roses for these structures unless you wish to remove the roses from the structures in the winter and cover them. The best choices are any of the Explorer Series climbers. If you do choose a tender climber, select a cultivar with pliable canes that can be easily tied to the framework and then relatively easily removed and bent to the ground in the fall.

John Cabot

William Baffin

'New Dawn' is a good rose for a pillar or obelisk; although tender, it is easily bent for winter protection. It is also easy to train horizontally along a fence.

Companion Planting

Roses make excellent garden companions to a variety of perennials, shrubs, annuals and even herbs. Good choices for companion planting are plants with contrasting leaf shapes and soft colours such as blue and white. Herbs provide the added benefit of deterring some pests and harbouring beneficial insects. Fibrous rooted perennials and vigorous self seeders should be avoided, as they will compete with roses for water and nutrition. The clematis is perhaps the best companion for roses as the blossom shapes are very complementary.

Clematis and Rose Combinations

Clematis are available in a wide variety of colours and can flower before, along with or after the rose. Clematis should be planted at least 1 m (3 ft.) away from roses as both have large root systems. The best varieties for Calgary are the viticellas and other class "C" clematis.

Clematis can be used to create interest in a rose bed by providing variety in height and bloom. Clematis can be grown up stakes or other supports such as obelisks which are placed in locations that will enhance but not overwhelm the roses. The colours chosen should complement the colour arrangement of the flower bed. For a bed of mixed rose colours, blue, purple or white clematis work well.

The mature size of the clematis should balance that of the rose; low growing clematis should be planted with low growing roses or the clematis will have to be pruned to size. Taller clematis are perfect for tall rose shrubs and climbers. Clematis can either climb up a rose or the two can share a structure. Some creeping varieties of clematis can be used to cover the base of roses.

1. **Mid to late season flowering clematis and early blooming roses**:

A clematis that blooms after the roses have finished should have light or bright coloured blooms. These blooms will show up best against the rose foliage. Suggestions are:

- 'Persian Yellow' rose and blue Perl d'Azur clematis;
- Yellow *R. primula* rose and Blue Angel clematis;
- 'Altai' rose and white Huldine clematis;

- *R. rubrifolia* rose and fuchsia red Mme Julia Correvon clematis; and
- White 'Kakwa' rose and dark pink Duchess of Albany clematis.

2. **Mid to late season flowering clematis and repeat or continuous blooming roses**:

When clematis and roses bloom at the same time, the colour of the clematis should complement that of the roses. Blue and purple clematis balance all colours of roses whereas paler coloured clematis are good choices for dark coloured roses. Clematis that are the same colour as the rose will create interest through the shape or size of the different blooms. Suggestions are:

- 'New Dawn' rose and White Huldine, Étoile, violet Violette or Blue Ravine clematis;
- English roses (any colour) and blue Arabella or blue *C. durandii* clematis; and
- White 'Blanc Double de Coubert' rose and white and blue Venosa Violacea or dark red Royal Velours clematis.

3. **Low growing clematis and ground cover roses**:

When matching clematis with low growing roses, choose clematis that have a scrambling habit. Suggestions are:

- Pink 'Nozomi' rose and blue Arabella clematis; and
- 'Heidesommer' rose and pink Alionushka clematis.

5 Establishing a Rose Garden

IN THIS CHAPTER, WE WILL DISCUSS everything you need to know to establish or expand a Calgary area rose garden, including:

- purchasing roses;
- locating and creating rose beds;
- preparing and conditioning soil; and
- planting roses.

Information on maintaining an established rose garden is presented in the following chapter, *Maintaining a Rose Garden*. Details on protecting your tender and hardy roses for the winter are given in the chapter on *Winterizing Roses*.

Keep in mind, as with any subject, different rosarians do different things for their roses at different times. Hopefully, we've managed to distill years of rose growing wisdom from many different growers into a form that is useful to you; however, if you choose to do something completely different that works for you, great! Our guidelines should provide you with a starting point that you can modify into whatever is easiest and best for your roses in your rose garden.

Purchasing Roses

In the dead of winter, most Calgary rosarians spend time poring over rose catalogues, investigating websites or reading rose encyclopedias and dreaming of how their gardens will look in summer, once the snow has melted for the last time. This is one of the most exciting times for a rosarian: selecting roses for a new rose garden or finding new ones to fill in empty spots in established gardens.

Choosing which roses to buy for your garden is an important decision. If you are just starting your garden, you should consider how much work you wish to put into the roses. Tender roses do require more maintenance and a lot more work in the fall than hardy roses but there is a wider variety to choose from. Many rosarians start out with hardy roses and add more tender roses to the garden each year. A good place to gather ideas is with the lists of recommended hardy and tender roses included at the end of this book.

Prepare a list before you shop so that you know what roses you want, and more importantly, how many roses can be planted in your garden. Have a few second choices ready in case your first choices are sold out, unavailable or unhealthy. Allow yourself only a few impulse buys, otherwise you will have to expand your rose beds or plant the extras in pots.

Roses can either be purchased online or from local garden centres. In general, roses ordered online are mailed to you as bare root roses and those bought locally are sold as potted plants. We recommend purchasing potted roses as they are usually larger, healthier and stand a better chance of surviving their first winter. They are slightly more expensive, but the extra cost is money well spent as life is too short to wait for bare root roses to reach full maturity. In many cases, however, the roses you want may be only available as bare root roses.

Most online rose nurseries ship grade A bare root roses. Roses shipped in pots will have a premium shipping rate and most nurseries will not ship them. Before shipping, the nurseries will ensure the roses are alive and healthy and if one of your selections did not survive the winter, the nursery will not ship it to you. It is a good idea to order a few extras in case this happens so you will not have empty spaces in your beds. Check your roses once they arrive to make sure they are all healthy; nurseries will usually replace roses that have died during shipping. Most nurseries allow you to choose the shipping date for your roses. Roses can be potted and started in a greenhouse or under grow lights, if they arrive before planting outside is possible. Roses shipped after planting is possible can be planted outside immediately.

Potted roses from a garden centre are recommended.

Potted roses at garden centres are sold in 5 or 10 litre (1 or 2 gal.) pots. Purchase the biggest rose bush possible but make sure it is healthy. A plant with dead canes, yellowing or browning leaves, visible insect infestations, or diseases should be avoided. If a rose appears to be dead or dying, it probably is, so do not waste your money on it.

Tender roses are available as either grafted plants or own-root plants (grown on their own roots). For the beginner rosarian, grafted roses are recommended as they are usually bigger and stand a better chance of surviving their first winter. However, one benefit of own-root roses is that if the plant dies to the ground during the winter, the plant can regrow from the roots.

Hardy roses are usually grown on their own roots; however, a small number of grafted hardy roses are available. Ensure that you are not purchasing one of these, as they are no longer hardy and will require winter protection. Grafted roses will have a large bump, called the bud union, on the stem between the canes and the roots, either above

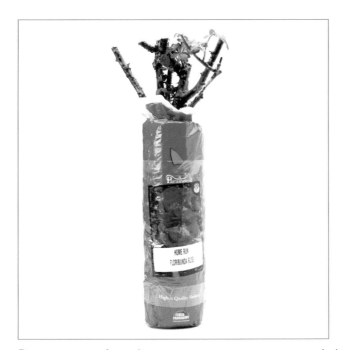

Bare root roses from discount stores are not recommended.

or just below the top of the soil. The bud union is where the named cultivar has been grafted on to the rootstock.

Locating and Creating Rose Beds

The location of rose beds in your garden is determined by the availability of sunlight. Roses require at least six hours of direct sunlight to thrive and bloom well. Southern exposures are the best. Eastern exposures are better than western exposures because eastern exposures are immediately heated by the morning sun after our cool Calgary summer nights. Northern exposures should be avoided.

Roses should be situated far from trees, particularly large conifers, which not only cast deep shade but deplete the soil of water and nutrients. Roses are heavy feeders and cannot compete with tree roots and very fibrous rooted perennials. Roses require good drainage and will fail in soggy soil. Avoid planting roses in low-lying areas of your yard, as these areas collect not only water but also cold air. Calgary's cool summer night air, caused by our high elevation, can slow rose growth and stress the plants.

Chinook winds present a unique problem to the Calgary gardener. The warm, dry winter winds stimulate growth that is damaged by subsequent freezing temperatures. The cycle of desiccating warm winds followed by freezing temperatures is the main cause of winterkill and death in shrubs in this region. To mitigate the effects of cold and wind, microclimates can be created by using barriers such as fencing and shrubs or by placing flowerbeds close to buildings.

Tender roses planted in a bed positioned against the foundation of the house may survive the winter better than those in a bed at the edge of your yard or in an exposed location. However, the roses will require more water in the summer because the eaves of the house will prevent rain from falling on the roses. The best location for foundation planting is a south or east wall. Do not plant roses against a north foundation.

Preparing and Conditioning Soil

Roses require well-drained acidic soil with lots of organic matter to thrive. In Calgary, this means that we cannot simply remove sod and plant roses in the uncovered soil as it is clay-rich, poorly drained, alkaline and poor in organic material. Any new rose bed must be prepared properly so that the soil is suitable for growing roses and the bed is visually appealing and easy to maintain.

The first step in creating a new rose bed is to "draw" it on the grass using a garden hose, rope or spray paint. In this way, adjustments to its shape, size or location can be made easily before any work has begun. Once you have finalized the bed outline, begin removing sod inside the boundary. It may be best to use a sod cutter if the bed is large and there is a lot of sod to be removed. Once the sod is gone, the soil inside the bed perimeter should be turned over to at least the depth of a spade (30 cm or 12 in.) and any rocks, clay lumps and roots should be removed. The subsoil in your yard may be a rich black soil, a silty soil with very little organic material or unsorted clay and cobbles. Due to soil disturbance during building construction, the type of subsoil may vary within the yard. Digging into the silt or the clay-gravel layer may be difficult but is necessary as without improvement, both subsoils will slow water drainage which could eventually kill any roses. However, if the subsoil is too difficult to dig, then raised beds may be the best solution.

Once the bed has been turned over, add at least 10 cm (4 in.) of peat moss and compost or herbicide-free organic material (e.g. grass clippings, leaves, etc.) and mix with the spade or a roto-tiller. Other materials that can be added to improve the soil include well-sorted quartz sand, zeolite, well-rotted animal manure, perlite and vermiculite. Every rosarian has a slightly different soil recipe but the soil produced should be light, crumble easily and have a high organic content. The upper surface of the bed when filled with amended soil should be higher than the surrounding lawn.

Fine mulch, consisting of wood chips less than 1 cm (⅜ in.) in size, can be applied to a rose bed after planting. It will help to retain soil moisture and discourage weeds from growing. The soil around rose bushes will require hand tilling during the spring and summer, either to work in any peat moss used as winter protection or to maintain the water basin during the summer. You may also need to move or replace roses throughout the summer. Any fine mulch can be moved aside for required maintenance and then easily replaced. Use of a coarse bark mulch or rock cover on rose beds is not recommended as it will interfere with regular maintenance.

Many rosarians will not only condition the soil in a new rose bed but also amend it as they plant roses. Planting is the best time to ensure the soil has the correct nutrients for your roses. As you dig a hole during planting, place the soil in a wheelbarrow or mixing area and add an equivalent amount each of peat moss, compost, manure or leaf mulch and 1 litre

(4 cups) of zeolite. Mix this thoroughly with a spade or hand digger and use this amended soil to fill the hole.

Planting Roses

Once your rose bed has been created and the soil is conditioned, it's time to plant your new roses. Both tender and hardy roses can be planted using the same process. However, potted and bare root roses, as well as own-root and grafted roses, have slightly different requirements.

Before any work begins, you should decide where each rose will be planted by arranging the pots or bare root roses in the intended bed. The two criteria that must be met are that tender roses should be positioned 60 cm (2 ft.) apart and hardy roses should be positioned at least 1 m (3 ft.) apart. It's a good idea to plant any tender roses together to make the winterizing process simpler, but this is not required as tender roses can be protected separately.

Depending on the size and shape of your beds, roses can be planted in a row along the middle of the bed, staggered in several rows, or somewhat randomly. Choose a fast growing rose, climbing rose, or the rose with the largest full-grown size as the focal point of the bed and place it near the centre of the bed. In a long bed, two or more focal points could be used; in a wide bed, several of the larger roses can be planted in the middle as the focus. Once the focus is located, the other roses can be arranged around it.

Some attention should be paid to the colour of the roses in the bed. Mixing roses of different colours will make each more noticeable, but establishing a complementary colour scheme may take some experimentation. Planting similarly coloured roses together creates a mass of colour to draw the eye, but individual roses may be hard to distinguish.

Bare root roses should be soaked in lukewarm to cool water for at least one hour before planting. Tap water is perfectly adequate, but rainwater is best. Do not soak the roses for more than 24 hours or the plants will drown. Potted roses do not require any special pre-planting treatment.

Once you have finalized the rose arrangement, begin by digging the hole for the focal rose. The hole should be about 30 cm (12 in.) wide and deep so that

Bed surface level

Water basin 5 cm (2 in.) deep

5 cm (2 in)

10 cm (4 in)

Bud union 10 cm (4 in.) below level of water basin

Step 1: Dig a hole 30 cm (12 in.) in diameter and 30 cm deep.

Step 2: Prepare the amended soil and replace about quarter of the volume back in the hole.

Step 3: Position the bud union and roots as shown.

Step 4: Fill the hole with the remaining soil, leaving a 5 cm (2 in.) deep water basin around the rose.

Planting a rose bush

as much soil as possible can be amended at the root level to promote healthy rose growth. Amend this soil by mixing in peat moss, manure and zeolite as described above and return about a quarter of it to the hole. If the rose to be planted is bare root, create a mound in the center of the hole with this soil.

Remove the rose from the pot or the water in which it has been soaking and ensure its label is securely fastened to the upper part of the strongest cane. Loosen a few of the roots and position the rose in the hole. If the rose is grafted, the bud union should be positioned about 10 cm (4 in.) below the bed surface level. Own-root roses should be positioned so that the lower portion of each cane is under the soil. Bare root roses should be arranged so the crown is on top of the soil mound; gently spread out the roots along the surface of the mound. If the rose is potted, ensure the rose is buried to the same depth as in the pot.

Once the rose is properly positioned, place the remainder of the amended soil around the roots and back fill the hole to the original bed surface level. It is nice to have a helper hold the rose during this step. Lightly compact the soil around the bush to ensure good root-soil contact. Scrape away sufficient soil at the surface to create a water basin 5 cm (2 in.) deep and about 30 cm (12 in.) in diameter; use the excess soil as a collar around the basin.

If you have a climbing rose and wish to use a trellis or some other structure as support for the canes, position the structure after planting the rose. Solidly embed the trellis or structure in the soil about 20 cm (8 in.) behind the rose. If there is a fence at the back of the bed, plant the climbing rose about 20 cm (8 in.) in front of the fence and attach the structure to the fence.

The last step in planting roses is to water them. Each rose should receive 10 litres (2 gal.) of water but do not fertilize at this time as you do not want to burn the fine roots on the plants.

❀ ❀ ❀

A STARTER GARDEN FOR ROSES

So, you want to have a rose bed or two in your garden but aren't sure where to start? The information in this box is for the beginner rose gardener in Calgary and summarizes how to create two simple and small rose beds with a variety of colour, blossom shapes, bush sizes and a succession of blossoms from spring to fall. All you need to do is to purchase the roses and garden supplies and follow the directions given.

Selecting Your Roses

This starter rose garden will contain 5 hardy roses and 5 tender roses, all of which are described and pictured in the two chapters *Favourite Hardy Roses* and *Favourite Tender Roses*. Two rose beds will be created: a 1 by 3 m (3 by 10 ft.) bed for the tender roses, and a 1.2 by 4.5 m (4 by 15 ft.) bed for the hardy roses. Bed dimensions and shape can be modified to fit your landscape or garden style and you can easily expand the garden by adding more roses. The two beds will require different fertilizing and winter care.

Hardy Roses:

| *John Davis* | *Adelaide Hoodless* | *Winnipeg Parks* | *Morden Blush* | *Thérèse Bugnet* |

Tender Roses:

| *Barbra Streisand* | *Secret* | *Olympiad* | *Iceberg* | *Apricot Nectar* |

Establishing the Garden

Detailed information on purchasing roses, locating and preparing your rose beds and planting roses is presented in the Establishing a Rose Garden chapter. We recommend that you review this chapter as the instructions below are simply a summary.

Ideally, roses should be purchased as potted roses as they are usually larger and healthier. Find the biggest, healthiest plants you can at your local garden centre. It can be difficult to find tender roses locally and they may have to be ordered online or you might have to select others from among those listed in chapter 15 *Favourite Tender Roses*. When selecting tender roses choose the grafted varieties. Hardy roses should be on their own roots and are readily available at local garden centres.

Start preparing the beds between April 15 and May 31. Choose the sunniest place in your yard, mark each boundary and then start digging. The beds should have the following dug into each: one bag of peat moss, one bag of cow manure and one bag of zeolite. Once the soil is amended, the beds are ready for planting.

The 5 tender roses should be planted in a row in the middle of the tender rose bed. Choose one rose to be the focal point and place its pot at the centre of the bed. The other roses should be positioned 60 cm (2 ft.) apart, two on each side of the centre. Placing the roses before you dig will allow you a preview of the finished bed. Plant the 5 hardy roses in the hardy rose bed, 1 m (3 ft.) apart due to their larger size. Use the remaining manure and zeolite to amend the soil used for planting the roses. Refer to the section *Planting Roses* earlier in this chapter for detailed planting instructions.

If you have purchased a trellis or an obelisk for the hardy rose 'John Davis', it should be solidly embedded in the ground about 20 cm (8 in.) behind the rose. If you have a fence, the trellis can be attached to the fence behind the rose.

Maintaining the Garden

Detailed information on maintaining your rose beds, including water requirements, fertilizing, pruning and disease prevention, is presented in the chapter called *Maintaining a Rose Garden*. We recommend that you review that chapter as the instructions here are simply a summary.

Your tender and hardy roses have slightly different maintenance requirements. The tender roses should be watered weekly during the summer. They should also be sprayed for powdery mildew and blackspot once a week. They should be fertilized 3 times a summer and, once a week, you should check them for aphids or other pests and deadhead as required. The hardy bushes only need to be watered every second week. There is no need to fertilize them as the amended soil contains sufficient nutrients.

a. long hose wand

b. hose, in-line spray bottle and short wand

c. spade

d. long handled loppers

e. secateurs or pruning shears

f. folding hand saw

g. hand trowel, straight and bent prong forks

h. gardening gloves

Winterizing

Detailed instructions for winterizing your roses are given in the chapter on *Winterizing Roses*. The tender roses should be properly protected every winter. Hardy roses should be protected during the first winter by mounding about 20% of a bag of peat moss at the base of each rose.

Beyond the First Year

After the first winter, the maintenance schedules presented in the chapter *Maintaining a Rose Garden* should be followed.

You can easily expand your starter rose garden into something bigger by adding more beds and more roses. Just remember to keep the tender and hardy roses in separate beds.

Enjoy your new rose garden!

Garden Supplies

The garden supplies have been listed below in sufficient quantity for planting and maintenance of the 10 bushes for one year. The necessary tools are also described. We've included directions to take you through purchasing roses, creating the beds, amending the soil and planting the bushes as well as spring, summer and fall maintenance for the first few years.

Assuming you already have the required gardening tools, the total budget is approximately $500; with $300 going for the roses and $200 for the supplies.

ITEM	AMOUNT	USE
Sphagnum peat moss	5 bags weighing 27 kg (60 lb.)	Bed preparation, rose planting and winterizing
Composted steer manure	4 bags weighing 18 kg (40 lb.)	Bed preparation and rose planting
Zeolite	4 bags weighing 10 kg (22 lb.)	Bed preparation and rose planting
Water soluble fertilizer containing micronutrients	One container	Feeding roses
Baking soda or milk	One box or one litre per month	Control of black spot and powdery mildew
Insecticidal soap	One bottle	Aphid control
Rain gauge	One	Measuring rainfall
Waterproof tarp	One tarp, slightly larger than tender rose bed dimensions	Winter cover for tender roses
Weights	5 to 10 bricks or light paving stones or whatever you have on hand	Anchors for tarp
Rose labels	10 robust plastic or metal tags	Rose identification
Trellis or obelisk (optional)	One	Support for climbing rose *John Davis*
Gardening tools	Hose, in-line spray bottle and long or short wand, spade, folding hand saw, long handled loppers, secateurs or pruning shears, hand trowel, straight and bent prong forks, gardening gloves, tape measure and a wheelbarrow.	

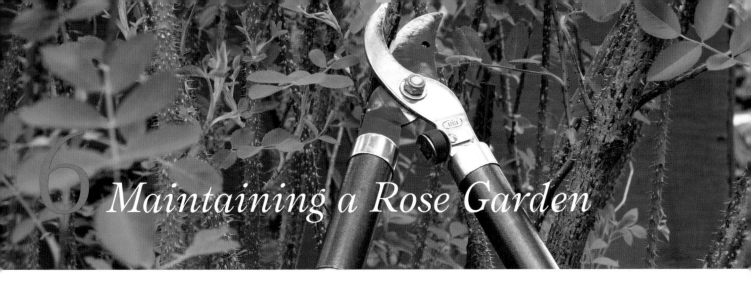

6 Maintaining a Rose Garden

A GARDEN FULL OF HEALTHY ROSES in full bloom is an unforgettable sight. However, this can take some work as roses do not thrive on neglect and are not plant-and-forget plants. Regular observation will prevent any serious problems from developing. Each time you wander through the garden, keep your eyes open for possible problems.

Maintenance items that can be dealt with on an *ad hoc* basis include monitoring plants for signs of disease or insect infestations, weeding, deadheading, pruning, defoliating and removing leaves from the soil. Watering and fertilizing should be regularly scheduled.

In this chapter, we will discuss everything you need to know to maintain a rose garden, including:

- water requirements;
- maintaining soil nutrients;
- chemical fertilizing; and
- pruning roses.

Information on creating a new rose garden is presented in the previous chapter, *Establishing a Rose Garden*. Details on protecting your tender and hardy roses for the winter is given in the chapter *Winterizing Roses*, which follows. Although we do touch on pests and diseases of roses in the maintenance schedule, more detail on these is presented in the chapters *Rose Garden Friends and Foes* and *Diseases of Roses*, respectively.

ACIDIC OR ALKALINE?

Is your soil acidic or alkaline? Slightly acidic soil is best for roses. Here are some simple pH tests for your soil.
- **Alkaline Test**: Pour some vinegar directly onto the soil. If it fizzes even slightly, your soil is alkaline.
- **Acidity Test**: Make a baking soda solution with distilled water, not tap water. Pour the solution on the soil. If it fizzes even slightly, your soil is acidic.

Watering Roses

Roses need a lot of water. Each average sized rose bush requires about 5 litres (1 gal.) of water per week, more in hot weather and less in rainy, cloudy weather. Roses grown in exposed, windy, or dry locations will need more water than those in sheltered areas of your garden. Rainwater collected in barrels is best as it contains fewer chemicals and has a lower pH which roses prefer. Otherwise, tap water can be used.

Roses should be watered in the morning so that the foliage is dry by nightfall. This will reduce the incidence of rose diseases such as powdery mildew and blackspot. If you do water the roses in the evening, try not to wet the leaves by directing the water at the base of each bush.

Care should be taken so that the water given to a rose does not drain away from that rose. This can be done by creating a water basin in the soil around the base of the rose, as described in the chapter *Establishing a Rose Garden*. The basin should be 5 cm (2 in.) deep, 30 cm (12 in.) in diameter and rimmed by soil.

Roses can be watered by hand with a watering can or a wand attachment on a hose. The advantage of watering by hand is that the water drainage around each rose can be observed and the amount of water can be adjusted so that little water is wasted. If water in the rose basin is absorbed in less than 5 seconds, the rose should be given more water. If water remains in the basin for about 15 seconds, stop watering that rose. Roses can also be watered with a sprinkler or drip irrigation.

Rainfall will reduce the amount of extra watering needed. A rain gauge can be used to record the amount of rain received in a week. Two to three cm (1 in.) of rain per week is equivalent to the recommended amount of water per week and means that you should not have to water your roses.

If you have a newly planted rose or new rose garden, we recommend that you monitor the plant or bed closely until you have an understanding of its water requirements. A rose may need more than 5 litres (1 gal.) of water due to its location, or it may never need more than 3 litres (0.6 gal.), even in the hot dry weather in late July and August. Check the soil around the rose and if it does not feel moist a few centimetres below the surface, the rose will need to be watered. If leaves at the base of the plant are turning yellow or brown and falling off, if the tips of the new canes are limp and hanging, or if buds are drying up without opening, the rose needs more water than you are supplying.

Nutrients for Roses

Roses are heavy feeders and need a lot of macronutrients and micronutrients to flourish. Determining the nutrient requirements of your roses as well as how and when to add these nutrients to the soil will ensure your roses are always at their best.

The macronutrient group is most important for healthy roses and includes nitrogen (N), phosphorus (P) and potassium (K). These will be available in the soil if it is amended as described in the chapter *Establishing a Rose Garden*. However, as the soil becomes nutrient-poor over time due to plant feeding, the nutrients will have to be added to the soil.

The micronutrient group includes sulphur (S), iron (Fe), magnesium (Mg), zinc (Zn), copper (Cu), cobalt (Co) and boron (B). In Calgary, iron and magnesium deficiencies are common as the high pH of both the soil and municipal water decreases iron and magnesium uptake in roses. Only iron, magnesium and sulphur micronutrients will be discussed in detail as they are most likely to affect the health of roses in Calgary gardens.

Nitrogen

Nitrogen is the most vital macronutrient for healthy roses as it promotes both stem and leaf growth. It is extremely mobile in the soil and is the fastest moving nutrient; it will reach the roots of a rose as soon as water percolating through the soil reaches the roots. However, too much water will flush any nitrogen through the root zone without making it available to the rose. Frequent application of nitrogen is therefore necessary, especially in the spring.

The best chemical source of nitrogen is a high nitrogen fertilizer. This should be sprinkled at the base of the rose and then watered in, following the package directions as to the amount required. The best organic source of nitrogen is alfalfa pellets.

A nitrogen deficient plant will exhibit pale lower leaves, wispy stems and undersized blooms. Over-fertilizing with nitrogen will cause roses to grow long, dark green canes with delayed blooming. Excess nitrogen will be exuded from the plant by a process called guttation, but this attracts aphids.

Phosphorous (Phosphate)

Phosphorous promotes flower and root growth. It moves very slowly though the soil, about 2 cm (1 in.) per year.

The best chemical source of phosphorous is dicalcium phosphate with an N – P – K number of (0 – 46 – 0) or triple superphosphate (0 – 45 – 0), sprinkled at the base of the rose and then watered. Bone meal is a good organic source of phosphorous although it takes years to benefit the plant.

A phosphorous deficient plant will have small blooms with dark green, light bronze or purple-coloured older leaves.

Potassium (Potash)

Potassium promotes the general health of the plant and aids in winterizing. It improves cell wall properties that enhance both water extraction from the soil and water movement within the plant. It also increases a plant's resistance to heat, drought and cold. Potassium moves slowly in the soil but it is extremely mobile within the plant, preferentially moving to the leaves, where it can be leached by rain. A final application of potassium in the fall will help to prepare the roses for winter.

The best chemical source of potassium is potassium sulphate (0 – 0 – 50) or potassium thiosulfate (0 – 0 – 25 – 17). The best organic sources of potassium are kelp emulsion, kelp meal and green sand.

A potassium deficient plant will have stunted buds with "burning" or "yellowing" of the perimeter of older leaves. A potassium deficiency looks very similar to frost damage.

Sulphur

The amount of sulphur in the soil controls the pH of the soil which in turn controls a rose's ability to access soil macro- and micronutrients. Roses prefer a slightly acidic soil with a pH of about 6.0 to 6.5 because at soil pH of 7.5 or greater, nutrients such as iron and magnesium become insoluble, fixed or underutilized. A simple pH test will indicate how acidic or alkaline your soil is and if it is too alkaline, agricultural sulphur or compost can be used to reduce the pH. Calgary's municipal water supply is alkaline with a pH of about 7.7, so if you water your roses using tap water you should test your soil at least once a summer to see if it has become too alkaline. Unamended Calgary garden soil has a pH of about 7.7.

The quickest way to lower soil pH (increase acidity) is to sprinkle ammonium sulphate (21 – 0 – 0 – 24) at the base of the plant and immediately water. Do not spray the foliage as it will burn the leaves. Well-rotted compost can also be dug in around the affected plants.

The safer, long term method to lower soil pH is to sprinkle agricultural sulphur on the rose beds. Agricultural sulphur contains 10% bentonite as a dispersal agent. Elemental sulphur is not recommended as it will take many years to affect soil pH.

Iron

Iron promotes photosynthesis, which controls the health of the plant. The amount of iron available to roses is dependent upon the pH of the soil. If the soil pH is too high, the rose will not be able to absorb iron; adding more iron to the soil will not help. Soil pH must be slightly acidic, with a pH of about 6.0 before the available iron can be used.

Iron is available in many different forms, but chelated iron is the fastest acting; it will improve the foliage in about a week. Chelated iron is a powder and can be mixed with water and sprayed on the leaves, as per package directions.

An iron deficient plant will have very pale coloured leaves, especially the young leaves near the top of the plant.

Magnesium

Magnesium helps strengthen cell walls and improves the uptake of nitrogen, phosphorus and sulphur. It stimulates basal breaks (formation of new shoots from the base of the plant), assists in stem growth and results in dark green foliage. Magnesium is an essential element in chlorophyll, the green colouring in plants. Slightly acidic soil will increase a rose's uptake of magnesium. The most common source of magnesium is magnesium sulphate or Epsom salts.

CHEMICAL FERTILIZING SCHEDULE: MAY – JULY

Modern Roses

May			June			July		
1	15	31	1	15	30	1	15	31

See Note 1. Fertilize 15 ml (1 tbsp) *plus* composted manure or compost 2 litres (8 cups) per bush. Fertilize 15 ml (1 tbsp).

Hardy & Rugosa Roses

May			June			July		
1	15	31	1	15	30	1	15	31

Fertilize 15 ml (1 tbsp) *plus* composted manure or compost 2 litres (8 cups) per bush. Fertilize 15 ml (1 tbsp).

Species & Old Garden Roses

May			June			July		
1	15	31	1	15	30	1	15	31

Fertilize 15 ml (1 tbsp) *plus* composted manure or compost 2 litres (8 cups) per bush.

Notes:

1. Begin uncovering these roses around May 1. The uncovering process should take about two weeks.
2. The minimum recommended fertilizing for each of the above three rose types is shown in the black text. The recommended fertilizer is 18 – 24 – 16 *or* 10 – 15 – 10 *or* 15 – 30 – 15 with micronutrients. Spread the quantity shown at the base of each bush and follow with the regular weekly watering or use as a foliar spray.
3. Water weekly (5 litres or 1 gallon per bush). Water after each fertilizing.

A magnesium deficient plant will have light green leaves with dead portions of tissue between the veins in more extreme cases.

Chemical Fertilizers

Roses are most commonly fed using chemical fertilizers available at garden centres. Both macro- and micronutrients can be added to the soil in rose beds by using man-made formulations with varying amounts of nitrogen (N), phosphorous (P), potassium (K), and micronutrients.

Macronutrient Fertilizers
The three macronutrients are listed on fertilizer packages in the following order: N – P – K. A ratio of 5 – 10 – 5 means that the mixture contains 5%

nitrogen, 10% phosphorus pentoxide (P_2O_5), and 5% potassium oxide (K_2O) by weight with 20% total nutrients and 80% filler material. Infrequently, there may be a fourth number on the package that refers to the percentage of sulphur; ammonium sulphate has the numbers 21 – 0 – 0 – 24.

- Nitrogen (N) is for green growth.
- Phosphorus (P) is for flower and root growth.
- Potassium (K) is for winterizing.

Macronutrient fertilizers are usually granular and are sold in large bags, the least expensive way to purchase macronutrients. The best way to apply granular fertilizers is to sprinkle them at the base of the rose bush and then water until the fertilizer is dissolved. Granular fertilizers typically cannot be dispensed by foliar spray.

CHEMICAL FERTILIZING SCHEDULE: AUGUST – OCTOBER

Modern Roses

August			September			October		
1	15	31	1	15	30	1	15	31

▲Fertilize 15 ml (1 tbsp).   Winter Fertilizer   See Note 6.▲
15 ml (1 tbsp).

Hardy & Rugosa Roses

August			September			October		
1	15	31	1	15	30	1	15	31

Winter Fertilizer
15 ml (1 tbsp).

Species & Old Garden Roses

August			September			October		
1	15	31	1	15	30	1	15	31

Notes – *continued:*

4. Potassium sulphate 0 – 0 – 50 (potash) can be added as a winterizing fertilizer and is shown in green text.

5. Ammonium sulphate can be added for extra growth and acidification of Calgary's alkaline soil. We recommend getting nutrient (N – P – K) and pH soil tests before adding ammonium sulphate.

6. Cover these roses during the last week in October or the first week in November.

7. Dates for applications are approximate.

Micronutrient Fertilizers

Some chemical fertilizers have the recommended proportions of macronutrients (N – P – K) and are enhanced with micronutrients specifically for roses. These fertilizers are typically sold in smaller quantities (usually buckets of 2 kg or 5 lb.) and are more costly.

These types of fertilizers can be applied by sprinkling them at the base of the rose bush and watering until they are dissolved. They are usually water-soluble and therefore can also be applied using a foliar sprayer.

Some micronutrients are available in chelated form that makes them more readily available to the plant. Follow the instructions carefully if you wish to spray your roses because some leaves can easily be burnt. Never apply foliar spray to rugosa roses.

30 ml fertilizer for 2 bushes

Fertilizer Application

We suggest that you feed your roses with a balanced fertilizer with N – P – K numbers such as 18 – 24 – 16, 10 – 15 – 10, or 15 – 30 – 15 with micronutrients.

The recommended amount of fertilizer should be applied around the base of each rose bush and watered in during the weekly watering.

The fertilizing schedule outlined in the previous table applies to all modern roses that are planted in your garden: Hybrid Teas, Floribundas, Grandifloras, Modern Shrub, and English (Austin) roses. These should all be treated the same. Miniature roses should be fed only half the amount given for regular sized roses. Once blooming Species and Old Garden roses do not need to be fertilized after blooming.

Pruning Roses

Pruning roses is defined as the cutting or trimming of rose bushes and is usually done in order to encourage growth. Pruning improves the health of the rose by removing diseased, dead, or damaged wood. As a result, the plant becomes more vigorous and increases flower production. Air circulation around and within a bush is improved by shaping the plant and removing crossed canes. Pruning can also be done to reduce the size or change the shape of a rose bush as desired.

Unfortunately, many rose references not geared to Calgary's climate and short growing season provide pruning instructions that are quite complex, resulting in the assumption that there are a lot of mysteries and rules about the art of pruning roses. While there are some guidelines that should be followed, pruning roses is easy. Even if you make a mistake, roses are very forgiving and it is extremely hard to kill a rose with bad pruning. An incorrectly pruned rose bush will grow and bloom. However, a correctly pruned rose bush will be a healthier plant and will give a much better display of flowers, so it's worth taking the time to prune properly.

In Calgary, most roses should be pruned in the spring, just as the rose buds begin to swell. However, roses that bloom on old wood should only be pruned in the summer after they bloom.

Roses only need to be pruned once a year but can be trimmed during the growing season to shape the bushes. This may be necessary, especially if a large climber or bush is threatening to engulf a walkway or patio area.

Pruning Basics

Make sure that you use clean and sharp tools. Thick, long sleeved gloves to provide protection from thorns and hand pruners are absolutely necessary. If you have large, old roses to prune, you may find that long-handled loppers and a pruning saw are helpful. The tools should be disinfected after cutting each bush to ensure that any diseases or pests are not passed from bush to bush. Use a weak bleach solution with 10% bleach and 90% water to disinfect your pruning tools.

Long handled loppers, secateurs or pruning shears, folding hand saw and gardening gloves

The following basic method is recommended for pruning roses in Calgary, although there are slight variations depending on the type of rose and the type of growth desired.

1. Examine the rose carefully before cutting. Identify any dead or diseased canes.

2. Remove the branches that look dry, shrivelled or black and remove all broken, dead, dying or diseased wood. The canes can be removed completely by making the cut at the base of the cane. Alternatively, you can prune the canes down to live wood by cutting off small pieces of cane until you see pale or yellowish green pith.

3. Once the unhealthy or dead canes have been removed, take a step back and re-examine the plant. Look for small, thin, or crossing branches, those that have grown across other canes. Remove any small or twiggy branches that are thinner than a pencil and then remove any crossing canes.

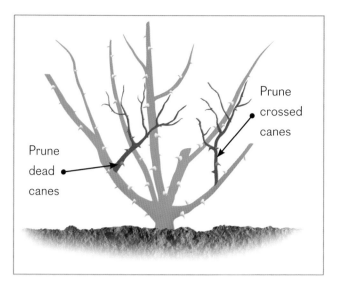

Pruning crossed and dead canes

4. The rose may look quite bare at this point, but you are not quite done. Each remaining cane should now be pruned so that the centre canes are slightly longer than the perimeter canes and the bush has a vase shape. Start with the outside canes and work inwards. Examine each cane before making any cuts and identify an outward facing bud near the top. Make the cut about 5 mm ($\frac{1}{4}$ in.) above the bud at a 45 degree angle. If it is hard to judge the distance, make a first cut about 1 – 2 cm ($\frac{1}{2}$ to $\frac{3}{4}$ in.) above the bud so you can see the cane more clearly. If you make the cut too close to the bud, the bud may die.

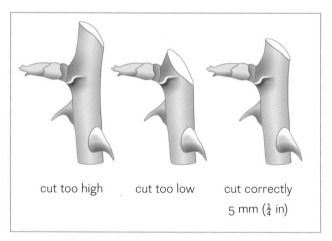

cut too high   cut too low   cut correctly
                                 5 mm ($\frac{1}{4}$ in)

Pruning canes at the right level

5. Once you have finished shaping the rose, take another step back. You will have removed about one-third to one-half of the volume of the plant, leaving healthy canes in a vase shape. The centre of the bush should now be more open.

6. The last step is to remove any dead leaves that remain on the bush as these can carry diseases.

Occasionally, on a grafted rose, the root stock will produce suckers from below the bud union. Suckers may appear as long, slender, flexible canes and must be removed or they will dominate the root system and kill the grafted variety. The best way to remove a sucker is to dig down to the root and tear off the sucker where it emerges. Cutting suckers off only encourages more suckers to grow.

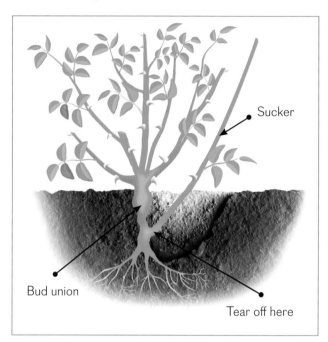

Removing suckers

Pruning Variations

The different classes of modern roses have slight pruning variations.

Hybrid Teas, Floribundas, and Grandifloras bloom best on the current season's growth. These roses should not be pruned in the planting year. The following spring, once the winter protection is removed, prune the diseased, damaged, spindly or crossing canes. Remove all but 3 – 5 healthy canes that are about 12 to 18 mm ($\frac{1}{2}$ to $\frac{3}{4}$ in.) in diameter. These should be evenly spaced around the plant to create an open vase shape and cut at different lengths to encourage continuous blooming.

Modern Shrub roses are repeat bloomers which flower on both old and new stems. For the first two or three years pruning is not necessary, except to remove dead or diseased canes. After a few years, the bush will need pruning to maintain its shape. Prune only in spring. Additionally, about one third of the oldest canes should be removed each year to prevent the bush from becoming an overgrown thicket of poor-flowering canes. To promote basal growth in English Roses, remove any non-flowering older canes.

In the first two or three years, climbers only require pruning to remove dead, diseased or broken canes. Climbers older than this should be pruned in spring to remove any winter damage or dead wood, but as little wood as possible should be removed. Older canes that produce few or no blooms can be pruned to the base of the plant, just before the buds swell. This renewal pruning will encourage basal growth. Climbers can also be pruned after the first flowering to allow the laterals to produce a second round of blooms. All side branches or laterals should be cut back to a dormant bud.

Old Garden repeat blooming roses, such as Bourbons and Portlands, flower on both old and new wood. These can be pruned in both the spring and the fall. The spring pruning should remove dead wood with the harder pruning and shaping done during the fall pruning.

Alba, Centifolia, Damask, Gallica, and Moss roses bloom once a year and produce flowers only on old wood. Pruning should only be done immediately after flowering in the early summer to allow the rose time to grow new canes which will flower next summer. During pruning, remove dead, diseased or thin canes and shape the bush.

Miniature roses should be pruned as the buds begin to swell. Prune dead or broken wood first and then trim to shape the plant and encourage new growth.

Deadheading

Deadheading spent blooms is a simple pruning technique that will encourage repeat blooming. It is only necessary to deadhead if the rose is a repeat bloomer or sets fertile hips. Once the petals have fallen off a bloom, use sharp pruners to cut the stem below the rose hip, above the highest 5-leaflet leaf set. If the hip is left on the bush, the rose will direct its energy towards ripening the seeds in the hip, instead of producing additional flowers.

In the late summer or early fall, deadheading should stop. This will discourage the rose from producing new growth that is easily damaged during the winter.

Cutting Roses

Cutting flowers for use in your home is also a form of pruning. Use clean, sharp hand pruners that have been disinfected, and wear thick, long sleeved gloves. Choose blooms that are one third to one half open to provide the longest display in your house, but do not cut flowers from young or frail plants. Ensure you have provided sufficient stem material for a balanced display in a vase. The cut flower should be placed in a container of water while you cut additional blooms. Once indoors, re-cut the stem under water at a 45° angle to prevent air bubbles from entering the stem. The cane remaining on the bush should be examined for an outward facing bud. Make another cut 5 mm ($\frac{1}{4}$ in.) above this bud to encourage new growth on the cut cane.

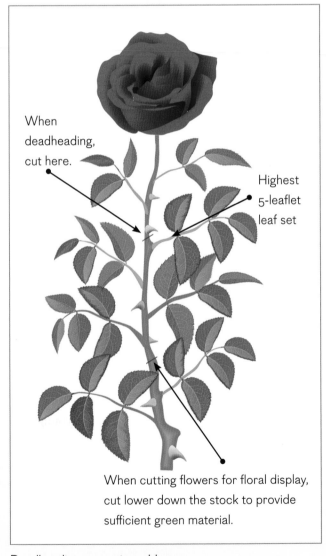

When deadheading, cut here.

Highest 5-leaflet leaf set

When cutting flowers for floral display, cut lower down the stock to provide sufficient green material.

Deadheading or cutting a bloom

7 *Winterizing Roses*

CALGARY HAS GREAT WINTERS COMPARED to the rest of the Canadian prairies; they're not too cold and we can always count on a Chinook coming in a week or two to warm us up. The bad news is that our winters are not mild enough to grow some roses without protection from the elements. As well, those warmer temperatures and dry winds that the Chinooks bring can desiccate roses and other garden plants. Protecting roses for the winter is an important consideration for Calgarians.

The amount of winter protection needed depends on the hardiness of any particular rose. We categorize roses as Tender, which require ample winter protection, or Hardy, which require little or no protection. Tender roses include Hybrid Teas, English roses, Floribundas, Grandifloras, Miniatures and any grafted roses. Climbing roses and Old Garden roses that bloom on the previous year's growth should also be considered tender roses. Hardy roses include the Explorer roses, Morden roses and some species roses. These roses only need winter protection for the first year or two, until established.

The location of your rose beds and the health of the roses will also determine the amount of winter protection needed. Roses grown near the foundation of the house will need less winter protection. Weak or unhealthy plants, tender or hardy, may not survive Calgary's winter no matter how much winterizing is used. The maturity of each rose bush will also control the amount of protection required; younger plants require more winterizing as they are still getting established.

Winterizing Objectives

The objectives of winterizing roses are:

- to prevent the temperature of the bud union from falling below −5°C (+23°F). Grafted roses must be planted with the bud union 10 cm (4 in.) below ground level to minimize frost damage of the critical bud union;
- to keep the temperature swings to a minimum. Roses should not repeatedly freeze and thaw in Calgary's Chinook winds;
- to keep the roses dry to prevent rot and freezing;
- to prevent desiccation as a result of Calgary's Chinook winds; and
- to prevent bugs, rodents and disease from surviving the winter on or with the roses.

Any method that achieves the above will result in successful winterizing.

Most of this chapter describes how to winterize tender roses but information for hardy roses is also included. We've illustrated a few different winterizing methods successfully used by Calgary rosarians to provide you with a choice of what to do. We've also detailed what to do in the rose garden in the spring when it's time to uncover the roses. These methods can be considered as starting points for you to develop your own personalized winterizing technique. The goal is to successfully overwinter your roses and have healthy, large and blooming roses the following summer no matter what method is used.

Winterizing Roses

We recommend that you do a few things before you even begin to think of winterizing. On or around September 1, stop deadheading. This will redirect the plant's energy from producing flowers to growing stronger canes. Around September 15, apply potassium sulphate to the roses to prepare them for winter. Make sure each rose receives a deep watering (about 10 litres or 2 gal.) sometime during October, just before the garden hoses are put away.

Winterizing activities should begin some time in the last half of October or the first half of November, depending on the weather. Roses can take a lot of

frost without impairing their growth so don't worry about colder temperatures before this. Wait for a hard frost and the warm autumn days that follow to winterize.

Protecting Tender Roses

The procedure for protecting tender roses is simple: add a first layer of dense insulation, add a second layer of lighter insulation and then add an outer cover. However, there are a few different ways of doing this and a few different materials that can be used as insulation and covers.

The steps for winterizing tender roses are:

1. Cut down roses.

2. Defoliate and clean up.

3. Sprinkle or spray sulphur, if desired.

4. Add peat moss.

5. Add leaves, if necessary.

6. Sprinkle or spray sulphur, if desired.

7. Add outer cover.

Rose bed and plant preparation varies slightly depending on the type of outer cover used. There are two main categories of covers: the first involves flexible outer coverings, such as carpet, tarps or foam (see the table and photos on p. 42). The second type uses rigid outer coverings, such as plywood or Styrofoam (see the table and photos on p. 43). Both methods are used successfully in Calgary.

Flexible covers require that the roses be cut down to 20 to 30 cm (8 to 12 in.); the roses can be taller but this will require more work as there is more rose to cover. If using rigid covers, the roses can be quite long, even up to 60 cm (2 ft.) if the covers are that high. However, the taller the roses are, the more material is required and the higher the cost of the materials. On the other hand, the longer the canes are under the protection the better, as there will be more plant available for new growth the next season.

The roses can be cut down with pruners, hedge shears or even electric hedge clippers, if you have a lot to do and little time. Once the roses are trimmed to the desired height, remove the cut canes. As well, any diseased leaves remaining on the plants or on top of the soil should be removed and discarded to reduce the number of insect eggs and disease spores that might overwinter. However, this is tedious work when done by hand and some may choose not to defoliate the plants. Alternatively, a shop vacuum can be used to remove the debris more quickly.

Rodents can be a problem as they like to burrow into the rose protection where it is nice and warm and eat the roses. Lime sulphur or agricultural sulphur sprayed or sprinkled on the ground and standing canes will deter mice and voles. As an added bonus, the sulphur will react with Calgary's alkaline soil to produce a more desirable acidic soil. Be sure to use agricultural sulphur as it reacts more quickly. This step, however, is not essential.

The next step in winterizing is to add peat moss to the base of the roses. Place a pile about 30 cm (1 ft.) deep around each rose. One large 107 litre (3.8 cubic ft.) bag will cover about 12 roses and can be purchased at a garden centre. For large numbers of roses, it may be more economical to have bulk peat moss delivered. If the peat moss is damp, it will need to be dried before being placed around the roses to ensure its insulating properties. A mixture of soil and peat moss can also be used but again, the mixture must remain dry.

Peat moss covering roses

Another option for this step is to place plastic cylinders filled with peat moss around each rose. The cylinders can be constructed by removing the bottoms from 23 litre (5 gal.) plastic buckets. The lids of the buckets should be replaced to help keep the peat moss dry.

The next step is to place leaves over the peat moss, although this can be omitted if the outer cover is Styrofoam (see *Styrofoam Box* and *Styrofoam*

Arches in the table and photos on p. 43). The leaves can either be loose or in bags, as desired. Straw can be used in place of the leaves but will be very time consuming to remove in the spring. Again, this layer of insulation must remain dry to be effective. Do not water the roses.

Once the peat moss and leaves are in place, more agricultural sulphur can be sprinkled on top. This will deter rodents from eating any exposed rose canes. If you have had mouse infestations in previous years, or live close to open fields, you may wish to use mouse poison to control the rodents. The poison should be placed in plastic pipes to prevent dogs or cats from accessing it. These pipes can then be placed around the roses, on top of the leaves or peat moss and under the top covering.

The final stage of winterizing the roses is to put on the outer covering and anchor with weights if needed. Then you can leave your roses until spring.

Climbing Tender Roses and Old Garden Roses
Climbing tender roses and Old Garden roses that bloom on the previous year's growth may vary in hardiness but require winter protection to preserve the flower-bearing canes and to allow existing canes to grow longer. The rose may survive without winter protection, but any exposed canes will die. Although new canes will grow from the ground each year, they will not produce blooms. To preserve the canes, they must be removed from any support, bent to the ground and buried.

These roses should be protected at the same time as your other tender roses, usually in the last half of October or the first half of November. The canes become more pliable after a frost, so wait until after the first hard frost. Detach the canes from their support and lay them on the ground, anchoring them with weights to prevent them from shifting during the winter. The canes should then be covered in the same manner as described above, with at least 30 cm (1 ft.) of dry peat moss and 30 cm (1 ft.) of leaves with an outer covering (see *Bend & Cover* in the table and photo on p. 44). Do not cut the canes, if possible.

If any of the roses have canes that are too stiff to be bent, even after a frost, they must be covered with the canes upright. Use the same method as for the tender roses, but cut the canes as little as possible, if at all. Unfortunately, these roses will not achieve the great heights that climbing roses achieve in warmer climates.

FLEXIBLE COVERING OPTIONS FOR TENDER ROSES

METHOD	PRE-COVER	ADVANTAGES	DISADVANTAGES	COST
Carpet	· Peat moss & leaves.	· Zero cost for old carpets.	· Not waterproof. · Moisture seeps through the carpet to form ice. · Carpets are heavy when wet and bulky to store.	· $0.00.
Tarp	· Peat moss & leaves.	· Inexpensive. · Easy to store. · Partially waterproof.	· Needs to be replaced about every 5 years to maintain water resistance.	· $20 to $50 depending upon size. · Available at hardware stores.
Micro Foam	· Peat moss & leaves.	· Light, thin (5 mm or 0.5 in.) and easy to handle. · Provides a very small amount of insulation. · Partially waterproof.	· Rips easily. · Micro Foam insulation does let some moisture through. · Mice will chew holes through it.	· $420 for 4 × 30 m (12 × 100 ft.) from a professional gardening centre.
Insulated Tarp	· Peat moss.	· Provides excellent insulation thereby eliminating the need for leaves. · Size and thickness (R value) can be made to order. · Waterproof.	· Large tarps are bulky to store.	· $177 for 4 × 8 m (12 × 20 ft.) with R4 insulation from a custom tarp supplier.

Carpet

Tarp

Micro Foam

Insulated Tarp

RIGID COVERING OPTIONS FOR TENDER ROSES

METHOD	PRE-COVER	ADVANTAGES	DISADVANTAGES	COST
Plywood Frame	• Peat moss & leaves.	• Solid and waterproof.	• Yearly assembly required.	• $8 for an OSB plywood sheet $\frac{3}{8}$ in. thick by 4 × 8 ft.
Custom Plywood	• Peat moss & leaves.	• Solid and waterproof.	• Yearly assembly required. • Manufacturing required. • Bulky to store.	• $8 for an OSB plywood sheet $\frac{3}{8}$ in. thick by 4 × 8 ft.
Styrofoam Box	• Peat moss.	• Provides excellent insulation thereby eliminating the need for leaves. • Flexible dimensions.	• Yearly assembly required. • Bulky to store.	• $22 for a Styrofoam sheet 2 in. thick (R10) by 2 × 8 ft.
Styrofoam Arches	• Peat moss.	• Provides excellent insulation thereby eliminating the need for leaves. • Waterproof. • No yearly assembly required. • Easily put in place and removed. • Can be partially opened (see inset).	• High cost. • Manufacturing required. • Bulky to store. • Beds must be sized to arch size.	• $22 for a Styrofoam sheet 2 in. thick (R10) by 2 × 8 ft. Polyurethane glue ($20 per tube) must be used on Styrofoam.

Plywood Frame

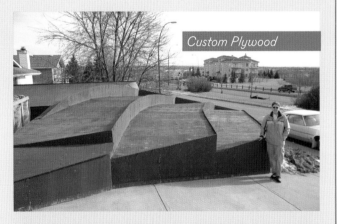

Custom Plywood

Styrofoam Box

Styrofoam Arches

METHOD FOR COVERING CLIMBING & OLD GARDEN ROSES

METHOD	DESCRIPTION	ADVANTAGE	DISADVANTAGE	COST
Bend & Cover	• Some roses only bloom on "old" wood. Accordingly, the canes of this year's growth must be preserved, because only these canes will produce blooms next year. After the first frost, begin bending the canes and hold in place with weights or pegs. Add peat moss, insulation (leaves or Styrofoam), a waterproof tarp and finally more weights.	• Preserve this year's canes for next year's blossoms.	• If a support is used for the canes during the summer, the canes must be disentangled from the support and bent to the ground. Be sure to use a support that facilitates easy disentanglement of the canes such as a solid post.	• $0.00.

METHODS FOR COVERING POTTED ROSES

METHOD	DESCRIPTION	ADVANTAGE	DISADVANTAGE	COST
Styrofoam Box	• Make a Styrofoam box similar to that pictured. Place the potted plants inside. Put the cover on. Secure with weights or fasteners.	• Very easy. Simply place the pots in the Styrofoam box.	• Yearly assembly required. • Bulky to store.	• $22 for a Styrofoam sheet 2 in. thick (R10) by 2 × 8 ft.
Trench	• Remove the roses from the pots. Dig a trench 30 cm (1 ft.) deep by 45 cm (1.5 ft.) wide by as long as needed. Place the roses in the trench and cover with soil.	• Yearly repotting enables newly amended soil to be used.	• Lots of work to remove the plants from the pot, dig the trench and bury the roses. • Roses must be repotted every year.	• $0.00.

Bend & Cover

Styrofoam Box

Trench

Potted Roses

Roses grown in pots on the deck or patio will not survive the winter in the pots in the open, no matter the hardiness of the roses. The pots can either be moved into a Styrofoam box (see *Styrofoam Box* in the table and photo on p. 44) or placed in an insulated heated garage. Don't forget to water the pots you have in the garage.

An alternative is to remove the roses from the pots and place them into a trench dug into the garden (see *Trench* in the table and photo on p. 44). The roses are then covered with soil. The roses can also be planted into a tender rose bed prior to it being covered for the winter.

Hardy Roses

Hardy roses do not generally require any winterizing. However, most benefit from some protection for the first one or two years until they become established.

The roses do not require any cutting or defoliating before adding protection. Simply mound peat moss around the crown or base of the rose to a depth of at least 30 cm (1 ft.). On top of this, add 30 cm (1 ft.) of leaves. Anchor the pile with a tarp or other water proof cover. Alternatively, bags of leaves can be placed around the rose on top of the peat moss. Once the rose has matured, winter protection is unnecessary.

You may find that hardy roses in an exposed location benefit from a peat moss/leaf mound each winter. The crown mulch may prevent winter tip kill which means a bigger and healthier rose bush the following summer.

Uncovering Roses

Rose protection should be removed in the spring, usually in April or May, depending on the weather. Do not be tempted to uncover earlier during a warm spell as any hard frost will damage new rose growth and any subsequent cold snap could kill the roses.

Tender Roses

A general rule of thumb for the timing of uncovering tender roses is to begin when the native poplar trees begin to bud. This is usually in the last half of April. The roses should be uncovered gradually, allowing them to acclimatize to the warm days and cold nights.

The first step is to remove the outer flexible or rigid cover and store it in preparation for next fall. Remove the plastic pipes and discard any remaining poison; wash the pipes before storing. Do not disturb the leaves and peat moss yet.

After a week or two, depending on how cold the weather has been, remove the leaves, but leave the peat moss undisturbed. Allow the soil around the roses to thaw in the warm spring sunshine.

In another week or so, again depending upon the weather, pull the peat moss away from the roses and lightly work it into the soil. Re-establish the water basin depression around each plant.

Regular maintenance should begin around May 15, or a week or two later if the weather has been cool.

Climbing Tender Roses and Old Garden Roses

The uncovering process for these roses should be started when the native poplar trees begin to bud, usually in the last half of April.

The same steps should be followed for these roses as for tender roses. The last step for the climbers is to re-attach the canes to the structure to which they were trained.

Regular maintenance can begin the same time as for the tender roses, around May 15.

Hardy Roses

Any hardy roses that were protected can be completely uncovered at the end of April when you start to expose the tender roses.

Move the peat moss and leaves away from the roses; they can both be worked into the soil around the rose or the leaves can be discarded or composted.

Regular maintenance should begin in mid May, with the other roses.

Winterizing Success

Roses can be considered to have overwintered successfully if green canes are present that do not die in the first few weeks after being uncovered. These will eventually support new growth. Although no green canes may be visible when you uncover the rose, new growth may start from below the soil so do not remove the plant immediately.

COLD HARDINESS

The original Species roses were found throughout the northern hemisphere in climates ranging from Sub-tropical to Arctic. To impart more winter hardiness to shrub roses, hybridizers have attempted crosses with the most cold hardy varieties. Among the species which have been often used in these attempts are: Spinosissimas found along the shores of Scotland, Rugosas from the northern islands of Japan, *Rosa kordesii* from Germany and many of the native roses of North America.

Sometimes over wintering seems successful, but the rose does not perform as it did the previous summer. A weak plant will produce few, if any, blooms so there is no advantage in nurturing it. If any rose has not achieved a height of about 30 cm (1 ft.) or has not produced several basal shoots by July 1, replace the plant with a better performer.

If you find that many of the roses in your garden are not being overwintered successfully, you may wish to modify the method you currently use. You could add more peat moss or leaves, use a soil and peat moss mixture rather than just peat moss, place straw bales or bags of leaves around exposed or raised beds, or use a different outer cover. You may also find that because of different micro-climates in various areas in your garden, you need to use different winterizing methods on each rose bed to achieve success.

If you think that winterizing tender roses involves too much work but still want to have tender roses in your garden, consider using one of the protection methods that reduce the work required. Insulated tarps (approximately R2) or Styrofoam (R10 or greater) preclude the need to use a second insulation layer of leaves. Once the tarps are cut and fitted to your beds, or boxes are constructed, relatively little labour is necessary to prepare the roses for the winter; you need simply to apply a crown mulch and place the tarps or boxes.

8 Growing Roses Organically

ROSES REQUIRE NUTRIENT-RICH, healthy soil to prosper. The required nutrients can be added to the soil using organic gardening methods, something that has been increasing in popularity in recent years. Organic gardening manages soil health by creating an environment that sustains microorganisms. A healthy soil that supports microorganisms may not need chemical fertilizers or pesticides.

In this chapter, we present everything you need to know to grow your roses organically, without recourse to pesticides or fertilizers. Information on preparing rose beds, preparing and conditioning soils and planting roses is included in the chapter *Establishing a Rose Garden*. The methods described therein follow organic gardening principles. The maintenance requirements outlined in *Maintaining a Rose Garden* are applicable to your organic rose garden, although the chemical fertilizer section should be ignored in favour of the information that follows in this chapter.

FEED THE SOIL – FEED THE PLANT

- Chemical and organic fertilizers should not be compared on the basis of the N–P–K percentages. Chemical fertilizers have significantly higher N–P–K percentages than organic fertilizers. However, organic fertilizers provide carbon-based material to feed the microorganisms and fungi in the soil. In turn, microorganism and fungi activity support plant growth.
- Chemical fertilizers feed the plant.
- Organic additives feed the life of the soil.

Organic Activity in the Soil

In the soil food chain, bacteria and fungi feed on plant root exudates and are in turn fed upon by protozoa and nematodes. The excreted waste of these microorganisms is then absorbed by the plant roots as nutrients. When the microorganisms die, the retained nutrients become available to the plants. Organic gardening manages soil health by creating environments that sustain microorganisms. A well-balanced population of microorganisms suppresses disease and increases the plant's defenses. Through their activity in the soil and their excretions, microorganisms contribute to soil structure and improve drainage and aeration.

A healthy soil food chain can be created by adding organic matter to the soil and reducing or eliminating the use of chemicals. Adding chemicals to the garden can reduce microbial populations, creating a need for chemical fertilizers. Fungicides used for treating disease will not only kill the disease, but also essential fungi, thereby removing important plant benefits. Any disruption in the soil food chain can reduce populations of large organisms such as worms. Consequently, soil structure deteriorates. Additionally, over-fertilized roses are more susceptible to insects and disease as fleshy plant growth is easier to penetrate.

Organic Fertilizers

Organic fertilizers are derived from any formerly living plant or animal matter and are carbon based. They provide micronutrients to the food chain and improve soil structure. Organic fertilizers feed the bacteria and fungi in the soil, provide numerous nutrients and minerals such as carbon and nitrogen, promote water retention, increase soil aeration, and reduce nutrient leaching into rivers and subsoil.

There are many organic fertilizers which will benefit your rose garden which can be obtained commercially or made in your garden. Although this is not intended to be an exhaustive and complete list, we will describe the most commonly available and discuss their uses in the rose garden.

Compost

Compost is organic matter that has been aerobically decomposed by microorganisms such as bacteria, fungi, earthworms and insects. Composting is a natural way to recycle organic matter.

Compost is a slow release fertilizer that provides trace elements such as iron, manganese, boron, copper and zinc. It also helps to buffer soil that is too acidic or alkaline. It has an N – P – K ratio that varies from (1 – 1 – 1) to (4 – 1 – 2).

Compost can be used as a mulch or top dressing for existing rose beds to an approximate depth of 5 cm (2 in.). Typically, compost is added in the spring, when the soil can be easily worked but it can also be applied as a soil amendment prior to planting.

A composter can be purchased at any garden centre but you can also build your own. The following outlines one way to create your own compost:

1. Two piles are recommended so that one will be composting while the other is being built. Place the compost piles in a sunny but discreet location. Calgary bylaws require a minimum placement of 1.5 m (5 ft.) from your neighbour's property. Each compost pile should be at least 1 m² (9 ft.²) to facilitate the decomposition process.

2. Organic matter such as dried leaves, grass clippings, soft plant prunings, fruit and vegetable trimmings can be used. Chop or cut the material into fine pieces to speed up the decomposition process. Do not add dairy products, oils, pet feces, weeds, infected plants, meat or any chemically treated plant material to your compost.

3. The organic matter should be layered as follows:
   a. Start with a brown layer: dried leaves or shredded newspaper to 5 cm (2 in.) thick.
   b. Add a green layer: fresh grass clippings, soft plant prunings, fruit or vegetable trimmings to 5 cm (2 in.) thick.
   c. Sprinkle compost, soil, bagged manure or compost starter over the green layer to introduce bacteria to your pile.
   d. Continue alternating the brown and green layers with introduced bacteria until the pile is 1 m (3 ft.) high.
   e. Once created, water the pile; keep the compost pile damp but not wet.

f. Heat will be produced in the compost pile by the active microorganisms. Once the organic matter is consumed, the temperature will decrease. In winter, the decomposition process will occur but at a much slower rate.

4. The pile should be turned or mixed about once every two weeks. Mixing introduces oxygen to the compost so that aerobic bacteria can live and reproduce. If not turned, the pile will be anaerobic (low oxygen), have lower temperatures, decompose at a slower rate and produce unpleasant odours.

5. Your compost may be ready for use in as little as 6 to 8 weeks. When ready, it will have a rich, loose texture that crumbles when squeezed but will not have an unpleasant ammonia odour. Using compost before it is completely decomposed may burn your plants.

Vermicompost

Vermicompost is compost created by the activity of earthworms in a controlled environment. Earthworms are nature's unique recycling machinery and their presence indicates a healthy soil. They live on organic matter in the soil and their castings contain many beneficial organisms, growth regulators, yeast, molds, humic acid and nutrients to improve plant growth and bloom production. On average, vermicompost has an N – P – K ratio of 0.5 – 0.5 – 0.3. Adding it to your rose beds will increase the rate at which other organic material will decompose.

Vermicompost can be purchased from local garden centres. Vermicompost can also be made at home as follows:

1. Select a bin about 45 × 60 cm (1.5 × 2 ft.) with a tight fitting lid to keep out pests and rain. Drill small holes in the side and bottom for ventilation and drainage.

2. Place moist, clean, shredded newspapers, dead leaves or peat moss inside the box and add about 1 kg (2 lb.) of red wiggler worms. Place some damp newspaper over the top to keep the material moist but not soggy. Cover with the lid and ensure the temperature remains constant, at about 20°C (68°F).

3. The worms should be fed small amounts of fruit and vegetable scraps. The amount can be increased gradually as the worms multiply. Do not feed meat, dairy, fat or citrus to the worms.

4. Monitor the progress of the compost as you feed the worms. Once the compost is complete and has a rich, loose texture that crumbles when squeezed, push it and the worms to one side of the box. Fill the other half with fresh starting material. The worms will gradually migrate into the new material to restart the process. Once they have migrated, carefully scoop out the compost and place it around your rose bushes.

Organic Tea

A tea, made with compost or alfalfa, provides all the benefits of the original organic material to the roses. Organic teas increase plant growth, suppress diseases and speed the breakdown of toxins by ensuring the nutrients in the original material and beneficial microorganisms are more readily available to the roses.

Organic teas must be brewed in a well-oxygenated environment to allow aerobic bacteria to multiply. Without oxygen, anaerobic bacteria will dominate the tea; these bacteria will produce alcohol that is harmful to plants.

Teas can be dispensed as either a soil drench around the plants or as a foliar spray. The tea should be strained before spraying to ensure the sprayer will not clog, but any filtrates can be spread around the roses.

Compost tea makers are available commercially but it is easy to brew your own:

1. You will need the following equipment: a minimum 23 litre (5 gal.) container, an aquarium pump, a hose and a bubbler. The hose should be connected to both the aquarium pump and the bubbler. Place the bubbler at the bottom of the container; a weight can be placed on the bubbler to keep it at the bottom.

2. Fill the container with water to within 5 cm (2 in.) of the rim; rainwater is best but tap water can be used if there is no alternative. Half fill a mesh bag or old pillow case with compost or alfalfa pellets and tie it shut. Place the bag inside

the container, anchoring it to the rim so it floats and does not sink to the bottom. Mix 30 ml (2 tbsp.) of molasses into the water to feed the bacteria.

3. Plug in the pump and allow the mixture to brew for 3 – 4 days, stirring daily to further increase aeration. The water should be a rich brown colour if it has brewed for enough time.

4. Once the tea is ready and you are ready to use it, stop the pump and allow the compost to settle. If you cannot use the tea immediately, continue running the pump and add more molasses to ensure the aerobic bacteria reproduce until you are ready. The used compost in the bag or pillowcase can be spread on the rose beds.

Rainwater

When it comes to watering roses, rainwater is significantly better than Calgary's municipal water as it has no chlorine and a pH of about 6.2 that is perfect for roses. Rain barrels can be used to capture and store rainwater which will not only benefit your plants, but reduce your water bill.

It is easy to connect a rain barrel to a downspout on your house or garage. An overflow pipe is recommended as the barrel will fill quickly in the summer rainstorms, but ensure the pipe drains away from the house. Placing the barrel on a pedestal of wood or bricks allows a watering can to fit under the

Rain barrel system

tap. A hose can also be connected to the tap to water the roses if it is raised sufficiently above the roses.

Several rain barrels can be connected in a row to capture as much rainwater as possible. A 3 cm (1¼ in.) plastic pipe should be connected and sealed to the base of each barrel. Drill a 6 mm (¼ in.) vent hole in the top of each barrel so that the water level will equalize across all the barrels.

Manure

The manure used in rose gardens should be well rotted or composted animal waste. Manure compositions vary with the animal species and feed used. Manure should be purchased from a reputable source as poorly composted manure can sometimes contain undigested weed seeds. Additionally, manure that is only partially composted may continue composting once placed in the garden and may burn the roses.

There are four types of manure commonly available to the Calgary gardener. Bagged cow or steer manure is generally well composted and will not burn the roses or contain weed seeds. Horse manure is usually poorly digested and may contain weed seeds. Chicken manure is usually high in nitrogen and should be used sparingly to avoid burning the roses. Sheep manure has low nitrogen but is high in phosphorus and potassium. On average, most manure has an N – P – K ratio of (2 – 1 – 2).

Manure supplies organic matter and nutrients to bacteria, fungi, earthworms and other organisms in the soil. The organisms will recycle the organic matter into forms that are readily available for plants to absorb through their roots.

Decomposed organic material will also help to improve soil structure or tilth by binding soil particles into aggregates or clumps. A soil with good tilth has good nutrient and water holding ability and supports root growth.

Manure should be used generously on rose beds as it feeds the life of the soil and improves the soil tilth. Poor soils with too much sand or clay will benefit from large amounts of manure. Manure should be added to the soil at least once a year, typically in the spring. It can also be applied as a soil amendment prior to planting and can be used as mulch on rose beds.

Alfalfa

Alfalfa contains a natural plant growth hormone, triacontanol, which boosts photosynthesis and increases cell division. In roses, triacontanol stimulates basal breaks, new growth from the bud union, which results in a vigorous plant with beautiful blooms. Alfalfa is more effective than many other fertilizers or soil amendments and is a good source of slow release nitrogen, micronutrients and minerals.

Alfalfa meal can be used as a component of an organic fertilizer tea, foliar spray or simply applied directly to the garden and watered in.

Alfalfa is available in pellet and in cube form. The pellet form is easier to use, but may be difficult to find in Calgary. A 25 kg (55 lb.) bag can be purchased at the Co-op feed mill and at some pet supply stores. Alfalfa pellets have an N – P – K ratio of 3 – 2 – 2.

Alfalfa pellets

Bone Meal

Bone meal contains phosphorous which promotes flower and root growth. However, roses are unable to access the phosphorous in bone meal directly. Over time, microorganisms and worms will release the phosphorous to the roses through digestive activity. Bone meal should therefore be treated as a very long-term source of phosphorous and no immediate effect on the plants will be apparent. If the soil food chain is not healthy and there are few microorganisms present to digest the bone meal, then the phosphorous will remain inaccessible. Bone meal has an N – P – K ratio of 1 – 12 – 2.

Grass Clippings and Leaves

Grass clippings and leaves are excellent ways to add organic matter to the soil. They can be placed directly on the surface of the rose bed; once dry and brown, they can be worked into the soil. The clippings and leaves will eventually break down to feed bacteria and fungi and in turn, feed the roots of the rose. A mulch of grass clippings and leaves will have an N – P – K ratio of 0.6 – 0.2 – .04.

Leaves will decompose faster if they are ground into smaller pieces. This can be done by placing them in an empty garbage pail and cutting with a whipper-snipper or by running over the leaves with a mower.

Kelp

Kelp meal is an organic fertilizer containing mulched seaweed. It is high in potassium with an N – P – K ratio of 1 – 0 – 8. The benefits of adding kelp to the soil are numerous. Kelp produces a slow sustained release of about 60 micronutrients, plant growth hormones (gibberellin and auxin) as well as vitamins and enzymes necessary for strong plant growth. The chelating ability of kelp will liberate minerals that are locked-up in the soil and make them available to plants. Kelp meal stimulates soil bacteria by increasing their fertility and is often used as a root stimulant.

Kelp can be purchased in liquid or granular form. It can be spread around the base of the plant, dug into the soil or added to the planting mix.

Epsom Salts

Epsom salts (magnesium sulphate) can be used in organic gardening although not organic in nature. As the salts break down, they will release magnesium and sulphur, both of which are usually lacking in Calgary soils. The importance of these micronutrients is described on page 33 in the section called Nutrients for Roses.

Blood Meal

Blood meal is a byproduct of animal processing. It is high in nitrogen (N – P – K ratio of 12 – 1 – 1) that promotes leaf growth and greener leaves. Blood meal proteins are also rapidly broken down by soil bacteria to form ammonia that provides nitrogen to the plant.

Blood meal should be used sparingly especially in warm, moist conditions as an overdose can burn plants or damage delicate roots. Applying too much blood meal means that the rose will grow foliage at the expense of blooms and roots.

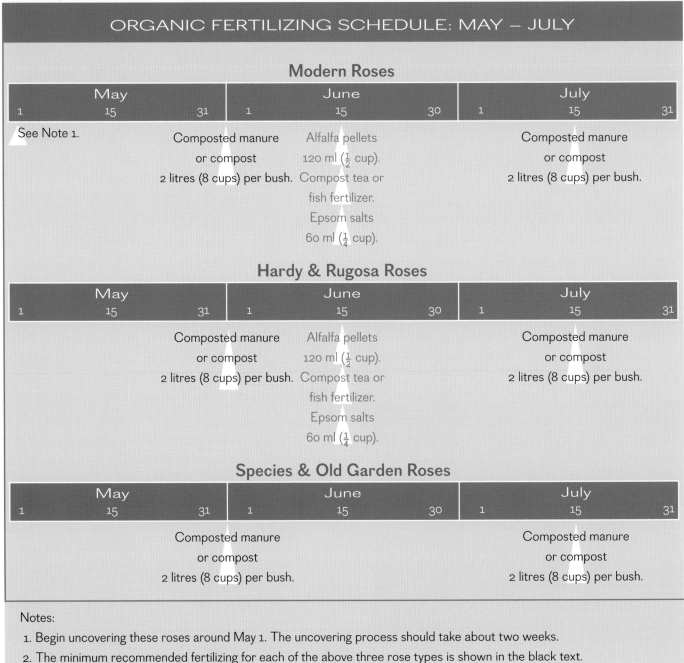

ORGANIC FERTILIZING SCHEDULE: MAY – JULY

Modern Roses

May			June			July		
1	15	31	1	15	30	1	15	31

See Note 1.

Composted manure or compost 2 litres (8 cups) per bush.

Alfalfa pellets 120 ml (½ cup). Compost tea or fish fertilizer. Epsom salts 60 ml (¼ cup).

Composted manure or compost 2 litres (8 cups) per bush.

Hardy & Rugosa Roses

May			June			July		
1	15	31	1	15	30	1	15	31

Composted manure or compost 2 litres (8 cups) per bush.

Alfalfa pellets 120 ml (½ cup). Compost tea or fish fertilizer. Epsom salts 60 ml (¼ cup).

Composted manure or compost 2 litres (8 cups) per bush.

Species & Old Garden Roses

May			June			July		
1	15	31	1	15	30	1	15	31

Composted manure or compost 2 litres (8 cups) per bush.

Composted manure or compost 2 litres (8 cups) per bush.

Notes:

1. Begin uncovering these roses around May 1. The uncovering process should take about two weeks.
2. The minimum recommended fertilizing for each of the above three rose types is shown in the black text.
3. Optional extra fertilizer can be added as shown in the green text.

Fish Fertilizer

Fish fertilizer is derived from processed fish byproducts. It contains important trace elements as well as nitrogen for healthy foliage and phosphorus for root growth with an $N – P – K$ ratio of $8 – 12 – 2$. In addition, fish fertilizer will acidify the soil.

Fish fertilizer is available either as meal or emulsions. Fish meal can be worked into the soil around a rose bush or added to the planting mix so that nutrients are released slowly. Fish fertilizer emulsions can be used as a foliar spray, which releases the nutrients more rapidly. Foliar sprays should be used either in cool weather, or in the morning or evening to prevent burning of the leaves.

The drawback of using fish fertilizers is that they can be extremely foul smelling and will overpower the fragrance of any rose. Odours will be reduced if the fish meal is well mixed with the soil or covered with mulch. Commercially available mixtures of composted fish byproducts and bark have a less powerful smell.

Certified Organic Products

Due to the increasing popularity of organic gardening, several commercial products are currently marketed as specially formulated, certified organic fertilizers with an Organic Materials Review Institute (OMRI) label. These organic fertilizers

ORGANIC FERTILIZING SCHEDULE: AUGUST – OCTOBER

Modern Roses

August			September			October		
1	15	31	1	15	30	1	15	31

Epsom salts 60 ml ($\frac{1}{4}$ cup).
Kelp meal.

See Note 5.

Hardy & Rugosa Roses

August			September			October		
1	15	31	1	15	30	1	15	31

Epsom salts 60 ml ($\frac{1}{4}$ cup).
Kelp meal.

Species & Old Garden Roses

August			September			October		
1	15	31	1	15	30	1	15	31

Kelp meal.

Notes – *continued:*

4. Water weekly (5 litres or 1 gallon per bush). Water after each fertilizing.
5. Cover these roses during the last week in October or the first week in November.
6. Dates for applications are approximate.

have different formulas, but in general contain alfalfa, fish emulsion, kelp, gypsum, rock phosphate and zeolite. They are available in both liquid and granular forms and are economically suited for small rose gardens.

Fertilizer Application

The organic fertilizer applications required throughout the summer in a Calgary rose garden are shown on the above chart. Most of the soil amendment takes place in early summer, with little required in August or September. Keep in mind that the dates shown are approximate and the activity can be performed from one week prior to one week after. The schedule applies to all roses that are planted in your garden. Hybrid Teas, Floribundas, Grandifloras, English, and tender Shrub roses should all be treated the same. Miniature roses should be fed only half the amount given for regular sized roses. The roses should be watered immediately after fertilizing in order to wash the nutrients into the soil.

ROSE DOCTORING – SOLVING NUTRIENT PROBLEMS

Even after amending the soil and using a regular fertilizing program, roses may still be deficient in specific nutrients.

To determine the deficient nutrient, examine the affected leaves and locate where on the plant most of the affected leaves are located. Plants have the amazing ability to move mobile nutrients from older leaves to younger leaves. Deficiency of a mobile nutrient will tend to appear first in older leaves (near the base of the plant) because the plant will move the nutrient from older leaves to protect younger leaves. Deficiency of an immobile nutrient will appear first in younger leaves (near the top of the plant).

Determining the deficient nutrient can be difficult because the symptoms are generally not as distinct as described below. Given that Calgary's soils are deficient in iron and magnesium, a simplified diagnosis is sometimes possible. If the younger leaves (near the top of the plant) show chlorosis (yellowing), then the deficiency is iron. If the older leaves (near the base of the plant) show chlorosis, then the deficiency is magnesium. Try fertilizing specifically with iron chelate (1 ml or $\frac{1}{4}$ tsp. per bush) or Epsom salts (120 ml or $\frac{1}{2}$ cup per bush), respectively.

NUTRIENT MOBILITY WITHIN A PLANT

Mobile Nutrients	Immobile Nutrients
Nitrogen	Iron
Phosphorus	Sulphur
Potassium	Calcium
Magnesium	Boron

Nitrogen Shortage

- Older leaves first (base of plant)
- Greenish brown leaves
- Some dead spots
- Smaller leaves and stems
- Severe shortage will effect all leaves

Phosphorous Shortage

- Older leaves first (base of plant)
- Dull leaves
- Dark green, with curled edges or purple tissue on underside of leaves
- Another indicator of phosphorous deficiency is small blooms that do not open readily

Potassium Shortage

- Older leaves first (base of plant)
- Light green leaves with brown edges
- Looks like frost damage

Sulphur Shortage

- Young leaves first (top of plant)
- Greenish brown leaves, stem reddish
- Difficult to distinguish from nitrogen deficiency

Magnesium Shortage

- Older leaves first (base of plant)
- Light green and dead portions (purple) in areas close to mid-rib between veins

Magnesium deficient leaves

Iron Shortage

- Young leaves first (top of plant)
- Light greenish yellow

Iron deficient leaves

9 Rose Garden Friends & Foes

INSECTS ARE EVERYWHERE, in our houses and even in our gardens. The insects in our gardens can be divided into those that attack and damage plants, those that have no effect and those that are good for the garden. Many gardeners tend to focus on the pests, but beneficial insects should be encouraged to live in your garden as they help to eliminate the pests.

This chapter will describe the insects, friends and foes, that are commonly found in Calgary rose gardens. Photographs of the insects and/or the damage caused have been included so you can easily identify what's living with and on your roses. We also discuss ways to attract our insect friends and natural methods to control or eliminate the foes.

The beneficial insects include braconid wasps, green lacewings, lady beetles, ground beetles and hover flies. These are discussed first. The pest insects and other garden foes follow; these include aphids, rose slugs, rose midge, cynipid wasps, rose curculios, spittlebugs, thrips, slugs, deer, rabbits, voles and mice. One benign insect, the leafcutter bee, is also included.

BENEFICIAL INSECTS

Braconid Wasp

DESCRIPTION: Braconid wasps are solitary wasps about 7 mm (¼ in.) in length and are either brown or black in colour. They have thin waists and long antennae. Their larvae are pale-coloured grubs.

REPRODUCTION: The female injects her eggs into the body of a host insect where the larvae hatch and feed inside the host's body. By the time the host dies, the larvae are fully developed and then pupate inside or near the dead host in a silken cocoon, to emerge later as adult wasps.

BENEFITS: The braconid wasp helps control aphids, sawfly larvae and caterpillars.

LURES: To encourage this wasp into the rose garden, grow plants that produce a lot of nectar, such as dill, fennel, parsley, 'Queen Anne's Lace' and yarrow.

Green Lacewing

DESCRIPTION: Green lacewings are delicate-looking insects with clear, green-veined wings and bulging coppery eyes. Their bodies are pale green and 10 to 15 mm (½ to ¾ in.) long. The larvae have sharp pincers and look like small, grey-brown alligators. Larvae often carry garden debris on their backs as camouflage.

REPRODUCTION: The female green lacewing lays tiny white eggs on long, silky stalks usually attached to the underside of a leaf.

BENEFITS: Lacewing larvae feed on the eggs, larvae and adults of aphids, mealy bugs, scale insects and spider mites.

LURES: Lacewings are attracted to plants that provide pollen and nectar such as goldenrod, coreopsis or 'Queen Anne's Lace'. Lacewings also appreciate a source of water.

Ground Beetle

DESCRIPTION: Ground beetles are large, iridescent beetles that are black, brown or blue. The abdomen is much wider than the front part of the body and most wing covers have faint lengthwise grooves. The larvae are pale, elongated, wormlike creatures with prominent jaws.

REPRODUCTION: This beetle lays its eggs in the ground. To prevent damage or disturbance of the eggs, add mulch on top of the rose beds.

BENEFITS: Both the adult and larvae of the ground beetle are predators and emerge at night to hunt cutworms, slugs, snails and other pests.

LURES: Provide rocks or other ground cover for the beetles to hide under during the day.

Hover Fly

DESCRIPTION: Adult hover or syrphid flies are yellow or white with black stripes, large eyes, tiny antennae and a flattened abdomen. They are 5 – 13 mm ($\frac{1}{4}$ – $\frac{1}{2}$ in.) in size. The larvae are grey or greenish in colour with a lighter coloured stripe down the back and resemble slugs or caterpillars.

REPRODUCTION: The adult hover fly lays a single white egg near a food source. The larva hatch within 3 days. They feed for 2 – 3 weeks and then pupate for 1 – 2 weeks, usually in soil, emerging as adults.

BENEFITS: The adult hover fly pollinates flowers and the larvae feed on aphids, scale insects, mealy bugs, thrips and leafhoppers. The larvae can often be found among the clusters of aphids on a rose as the aphids will not recognize it as a predator. A single hover fly larva will exterminate an entire cluster of aphids and then move on to the next.

LURES: Attract hover flies by providing sources of nectar such as goldenrod, yarrow, coreopsis, gaillardia or coneflower.

Lady Beetle

DESCRIPTION: Lady beetles or ladybugs are round or oval-shaped insects. They range in colour from pale yellow to dark red. Many have spots. Their larvae look like little spiny, black alligators with yellow and white spots. The two-spotted lady beetle is the most common lady beetle found in Alberta.

REPRODUCTION: Lady beetles lay their tiny yellow eggs in clusters on the underside of leaves or petals.

BENEFITS: Lady beetles and their larva are avid predators of aphids, scale, insects, mites and whiteflies.

LURES: Attract lady beetles by planting butterfly weed, goldenrod, yarrow and 'Queen Anne's Lace' as well as herbs like fennel, dill or coriander. Lady beetles overwinter as adults under piles of leaf litter or in other protected spaces so leave piles of mulch in the garden. This mulch should be removed in late spring when the beetles need no longer need the protection from spring frosts.

BENIGN INSECTS

Leafcutter Bees

DESCRIPTION: Leafcutter bees are solitary bees about the size of the common honeybee. They are not aggressive and will not sting unless handled.

REPRODUCTION: Leafcutter bees nest in soft rotten wood or the stems of plants. They collect pieces of leaves to construct nest cells into which the females lay eggs. There is only one generation per year. Leafcutter bees are most active in June and July.

DAMAGE: Leafcutter bees are important pollinators, however the damage they do to rose leaves can be unsightly. They prefer roses with soft, smooth leaves such as 'John Cabot', 'William Baffin' and any Albas.

CONTROL: The damage by leafcutter bees will not harm the plant. To protect the leaves from leafcutter bees, cover the rose with cheesecloth or other loose netting.

INSECT PESTS

Aphids

DESCRIPTION: Aphids are small, pear-shaped, soft-bodied insects with long legs and antenna. They are generally brown or green. They are often found in large colonies on new growth or around new buds.

REPRODUCTION: In the fall, aphids deposit their eggs on rose canes and the eggs hatch in the spring. Rose aphids reproduce asexually, with adult females giving birth to live nymphs that are already pregnant.

DAMAGE: Aphids suck sap from plants with needle-like mouths. Large populations of aphids can result in reduced growth and wilted leaves.

CONTROL: Aphids can be controlled by knocking them off the bush with a spray of water, by rubbing or squashing them or by attracting their natural enemies to the garden. Spraying with insecticidal soap or Pyrethrum will kill aphids and spraying the plants in the fall with dormant oil will kill over-wintering eggs. Avoid excess nitrogen fertilizer as it will cause vigorous growth of soft stem and bud tissue, which attracts aphids.

Cynipid Wasps

DESCRIPTION: Cynipid wasps, also known as rose gall wasps, are small dark coloured insects between 3 and 9 mm ($\frac{1}{8}$ to $\frac{3}{8}$ in.) in length. They have narrow waists and long antennae.

REPRODUCTION: Cynipid wasps reproduce asexually. The female lays eggs inside the stem or along the stem of a rose. The plant then grows a fuzzy gall and the larvae develop inside, protected from predators.

DAMAGE: The interaction between the insect and the rose induces the rose to grow a gall. Rose galls can look like fuzzy balls, dried nuts or berries but do not affect the plant. They are very commonly found on native wild roses in the Calgary area.

CONTROL: Cynipid wasps can be controlled by cutting off the infected cane below the gall and destroying it. However, removing the galls may not totally eliminate problems if adult wasps fly in from nearby areas.

Rose Curculio

DESCRIPTION: The rose curculio is a shiny, red weevil about 8 mm ($\frac{3}{8}$ in.) in length with a long black snout. It can fly from rose to rose but very awkwardly. The legless larvae are white and about 1 mm ($\frac{1}{16}$ in.) in length.

REPRODUCTION: The female lays her eggs in the developing rose flowers and the larvae feed on the reproductive parts of the rose. When fully grown, the larvae fall to the ground to pupate in the soil over the winter. They emerge as adults in late spring to early summer. The rose curculio has one generation each year.

DAMAGE: Rose curculio feed on all types of roses, especially shrub roses, by chewing holes through the side of the flower buds. This causes the buds to wilt and possibly die; any resulting flowers will be deformed or full of holes.

CONTROL: To control rose curculio, pick the adults off the blooms and squish them. Remove damaged buds and spent blossoms. The affected plant can be shaken over a bucket of soapy water, which causes the weevils to drop into the water and drown.

Rose Midge

DESCRIPTION: Rose midge are small, delicate flies about 2 mm ($\frac{1}{8}$ in.) in length. The larvae are reddish in colour and about 2 mm long. The adults emerge in early spring from pupae in the soil.

REPRODUCTION: Females lay their eggs inside rose buds or the tips of emerging leaves. Once hatched, the larvae begin feeding on the sap from the forming bud. There are several generations per year and a single generation can be as short as two weeks.

DAMAGE: Once the midge leave the damaged tips, the buds wither, blacken, and die. An infestation of midge can cause complete failure of a bloom cycle, leaving a rose bed filled with what appear to be blind shoots.

CONTROL: Control midge by cutting off the affected shoot; ensure enough of the stem is removed to eliminate all larvae. Insecticidal soaps can be used to control midge populations. Azadirachtin neem extract, not neem oil, is also effective against midge.

Rose Slugs

DESCRIPTION: Rose slugs are the larvae of wasps called sawflies; the ones commonly seen in Calgary gardens are the European rose slugs *Endelomyia aethiops*. These larvae are light green with brownish-orange heads and range in size from 6 to 12 mm ($\frac{1}{4} - \frac{1}{2}$ in.) in length. Adult sawflies are shiny black stout-bodied wasps about 5 mm ($\frac{1}{4}$ in.) long.

REPRODUCTION: Female sawflies lay eggs along the margins of leaves. When the young hatch, they feed on the leaves. Once fully grown, the rose slug drops to the ground and pupates in the soil. Sawflies produce one generation per year.

DAMAGE: Rose slugs are especially destructive in late June. They will consume the green part of the leaf, leaving a skeleton that eventually turns brown. The damage to the leaves interferes with photosynthesis that weakens the plant.

CONTROL: Control rose slugs either by hand picking the larva from the underside of the leaves and squashing them or spraying the infested bushes with insecticidal soap or horticultural oil. Ensure that the bottoms of the leaves are well-coated as this is where the rose slugs feed.

Slugs

DESCRIPTION: Slugs found in Calgary gardens are European imports, *Deroceras reticulatumin*, related to snails and clams. They are light gray in colour and leave a shiny trail of mucus. They need moisture to thrive and hide during the day in dark, damp places.

REPRODUCTION: Slugs lay their eggs in the soil and emerge in the spring, reaching maturity in about 4 months.

DAMAGE: Slugs emerge at night to feed on plants, eating holes in the leaves and flowers.

CONTROL: To control slugs, sprinkle crushed eggshells or diatomaceous earth around susceptible plants; this will damage the slugs' bodies as they crawl across the barrier. This treatment should be reapplied after rain or soil disturbance. Copper scrub pads will also deter slugs. A saucer of beer will attract slugs, which will then drown in the beer. New commercial slug baits made from iron phosphate can be used; however, this pesticide can be toxic to organisms in the soil. The European ground beetle is the only natural enemy of slugs.

Beneficial Insects:	Braconid Wasp	Green Lacewing	Lady Beetle	Ground Beetle	Hover Fly
Attracting Plants (below):					
Alyssum		✿			
Amaranthus				✿	
Coreopsis		✿			✿
Cosmos					✿
Dill	✿	✿	✿		
Dwarf Morning Glory			✿		
Fennel	✿		✿		
Fernleaf Yarrow	✿	✿	✿		
Lupin					✿
Parsley	✿				
Pincushion flower					✿
Queen Anne's Lace	✿	✿	✿		✿

Spittlebugs

DESCRIPTION: Spittlebugs are leaf-sucking insects related to leafhoppers. The adults are tan or brown in colour with blunt heads and large eyes and are about 6 mm (¼ in.) long. Spittlebugs are usually seen in the nymph stage surrounded by a mass of sticky, frothy bubbles.

REPRODUCTION: Spittlebugs overwinter as eggs in plant debris. The eggs hatch in spring and the orange nymph begins to feed and froth. A nymph can molt four times and emerges from the froth as an adult in early summer. Only one generation is produced each year.

DAMAGE: Spittlebug adults and nymphs suck plant juices but are rarely a serious problem.

CONTROL: Spittlebugs can be controlled through spraying the froth away with water. This exposes the nymph to its predator, the yellow jacket. Fall and winter cleanup of fallen leaves helps prevent eggs from overwintering.

Thrips

DESCRIPTION: Thrips are tiny, quick moving insects about 1 mm ($\frac{1}{16}$ in.) in length. They are dark brown in colour with four narrow, fuzzy wings. The nymphs are the same size and shape, but do not have wings and are yellowish brown in colour.

REPRODUCTION: Female thrips lay eggs, which hatch in two to seven days, in leaf tissue. The nymphs have two nymphal stages followed by two pupa stages either on the plant or in the soil. Thrips have a life cycle of about two weeks.

DAMAGE: Thrips attack rose buds just as they are opening by sucking out the sap. As a result, the bloom either will not open or will only partially open as a distorted flower with brown edges. Thrips prefer hot and dry conditions and light coloured flowers. They are active from late spring to midsummer.

CONTROL: To control thrips, remove infected buds or wash the thrips off with water. Thrips will also be repelled by plants of the onion family. In addition, lady beetles, lacewings and other beetles eat thrips.

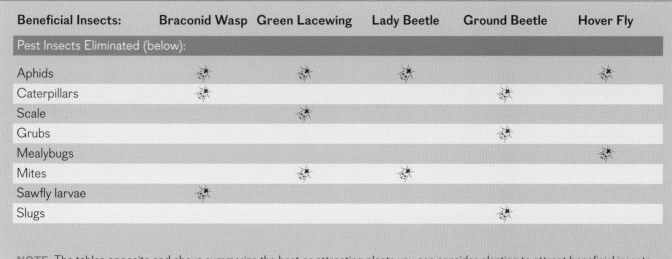

Beneficial Insects:	Braconid Wasp	Green Lacewing	Lady Beetle	Ground Beetle	Hover Fly
Pest Insects Eliminated (below):					
Aphids	🐞	🐞	🐞		🐞
Caterpillars	🐞			🐞	
Scale		🐞			
Grubs				🐞	
Mealybugs					🐞
Mites		🐞	🐞		
Sawfly larvae	🐞				
Slugs				🐞	

NOTE: The tables opposite and above summarize the host or attracting plants you can consider planting to attract beneficial insects into your garden and the insect pests that these beneficial insects prey upon and help eliminate.

MAMMAL & RODENT PESTS

Deer & Rabbits

DAMAGE: Deer and rabbits love to eat roses, especially new buds and growth. Nothing can decimate a rose garden faster than a hungry deer. Deer are less of a problem in the inner city as there are not as many as in rural areas. Calgary's population of snowshoe hares is most active in the rose garden in winter and early spring. The roses will most likely recover from a rabbit or deer attack, but they will not be at their best for a few years.

CONTROL: A 2.4 m (8.0 ft.) high electric fence is the most effective way to discourage deer. Some commercial products that claim to discourage deer are also available. Chicken wire can be placed around roses to keep rabbits away but it is unsightly.

Voles & Mice

DAMAGE: Voles and mice attack roses by eating the roots or chewing off the bark. The worst damage occurs in the winter when the protective covering on top of tender roses gives these pests a nice warm place to live. Little hills or lines in the snow indicate the presence of these critters. Voles and field mice build their nests in compost heaps, piles of leaves and pots.

CONTROL: Before covering roses for the winter, sprinkle sulphur on the ground to deter voles and mice. Bait and traps will work but make sure they are in areas away from children and pets.

POWDERY MILDEW CONTROL

The best advice is the old saying "An ounce of prevention is worth a pound of cure". Once roses have mildew, it is nearly impossible to eliminate, so treat your roses as if they have mildew even when they don't.

Fungicides are a chemical method of controlling powdery mildew. Milk, sodium bicarbonate (baking soda) and potassium bicarbonate can be used as non-toxic sprays to prevent and control powdery mildew. A sulphur solution can also be used, but spray lightly as excess sulphur will kill beneficial soil fungi.

Some gardeners alternate use of these treatments to greater effectiveness than using a single treatment.

Treatment	Disease Controlled	Recipe (hand sprayer)*	Frequency
Fungicides (Funginex)	• Powdery Mildew • Black Spot	5 ml per litre of water	Spray every 7 days
Milk	• Powdery Mildew	1 part milk to 9 parts water	Spray every 7 days
Sodium Bicarbonate Potassium Bicarbonate	• Powdery Mildew • Black Spot	15 ml of bicarbonate + 15 ml insecticidal soap per litre of water	Spray every 7 to 14 days
Sulphur	• Powdery Mildew	22 ml sulphur + 45 ml horticulture oil per 5 litres of water	Spray lightly every 7 to 14 days

* If you have more than 20 roses, a hand sprayer (orange and green topped bottle at lower left) may be inadequate and a pressure sprayer (below, right) may be preferred. For even larger rose gardens, a hose end sprayer (yellow topped bottle at upper left) will be faster. When using a hose end sprayer, the mixtures must be more concentrated than the hand sprayer recipe shown above because of the diluting effect of the hose water. Please follow directions carefully when using either hand sprayers or hose end sprayers.

Sodium bicarbonate (baking soda) and potassium bicarbonate are both equally effective against mildew and blackspot. However, baking soda can hamper the absorption of iron, magnesium and calcium if used over a period of years. Potassium bicarbonate solutions have no undesirable effects. While baking soda is perfect for the occasional spraying, keep it in the kitchen for the long haul and use potassium bicarbonate in the garden.

Powdery mildew

IO Diseases of Roses

LIKE MANY OTHER BEAUTIFUL PLANTS, roses can be affected by diseases. Some of these diseases only attack roses whereas others can run rampant though your garden, affecting your roses only because they are there. The good news is that these diseases can be fought and controlled.

There are three main types of diseases that affect roses: fungal, bacterial and viral. Of these, fungal diseases are the most serious. In this chapter, we discuss the nature, symptoms and methods of disease control so you can recognize and mitigate them. In addition to diseases, we've also included information on growth mutations that may be observed on your roses.

The diseases are listed in alphabetical order, with three exceptions. Powdery mildew, blackspot and rust are discussed first because they are the three most severe fungal diseases that can attack your roses.

Powdery Mildew

DESCRIPTION: Powdery mildew is caused by the fungus *Sphaerotheca pannosa* that lives on the outer surfaces of leaves. The fungus sends little shoots into the cells of the leaf, disfiguring and weakening the plant. The young leaves curl and twist as they develop, while older leaves will show a white powdery dusting where the outbreak is severe.

Cloudy, humid weather with warm days and cool nights are ideal conditions for mildew to become established. This is particularly true in Calgary where late afternoon showers and cool nights are common. It takes 7 to 10 days from the time the mildew fungus lands on a leaf for the symptoms to appear.

DAMAGE: Powdery mildew usually attacks the lower surface of the leaf first and then appears on the top of the leaf. Infected flower buds become distorted as they open but mature flowers are seldom affected.

CONTROL: To decrease the chances of mildew, plant disease resistant rose varieties. Ensure that the roses have adequate ventilation. Plant roses in full sunlight and water early in the day to ensure the leaves dry before nightfall. Avoid chemical fertilizers high in nitrogen as these promote succulent growth that is susceptible to both disease and insects. Feed the roses organically so they develop a thicker cuticle on leaf surfaces and are therefore less susceptible to fungal disease.

To help control powdery mildew, prepare a solution of sodium or potassium bicarbonate and insecticidal soap. Beginning as soon as rose buds appear in the spring, spray the plants every 7 to 14 days. Spraying with a fungicide, milk or sulphur may also be effective. More details are given in the previous feature on Powdery Mildew Control appearing before chapter 10.

In the fall, pick up and prune out infected leaves before adding winter protection to reduce the chances of powdery mildew spores over-wintering.

Black Spot

DESCRIPTION: Black spot is a serious disease that affects many types of roses. It is caused by the fungus *Diplocarpon rosea* which lives on rose leaves, in leaf litter and on infected rose canes. The spores of the fungus are spread by wind or splashing water. The abundance of black spot varies from year to year and is more common later in the summer. Black spot appears as black circular spots that can grow up to 10 mm ($\frac{1}{2}$ in.) in diameter, usually during periods of wet weather. The spores germinate when they have been wet for at least 7 hours and the temperature is around 18°–24°C (65°–75°F).

DAMAGE: The lower leaves of a rose bush become infected first. The disease then spreads to the entire plant causing yellowing of the leaves and defoliation. Black spot weakens the plant and, if left unchecked, the plant may die.

CONTROL: Plant roses in locations that reduce favourable conditions for the development of black spot. Ensure that there is adequate air circulation among the roses. The foliage of roses planted in full sunlight will dry rapidly once wet. Avoid wetting the foliage when watering roses, especially during dark, cloudy days. Plant black spot resistant varieties of roses.

During the summer, infected leaves can be removed from the rose and from the soil around the rose and discarded. Prune and discard any infected stems. A solution of sodium or potassium bicarbonate can be used to spray the infected plants every 7 to 14 days. A systemic fungicide can be used for extreme outbreaks. In the fall, pick up and prune out infected leaves and stems before adding winter protection to reduce the chances of black spot spores over-wintering.

Rust

DESCRIPTION: Rust is caused by a fungus called *Phragmidium mucronatum* and appears as red-orange spots on the undersides of leaves, on hips and at leaf axels. It can also appear on young rose canes as long narrow spots or streaks. Rust thrives in cool, moist weather (18°–21°C, 64°–69°F). The spores reproduce every 10 to 14 days throughout summer and are spread by insects, rain and wind.

DAMAGE: If left unchecked, this disease can cause defoliation of the entire rose plant.

CONTROL: As soon as signs of rust appear, infected leaves and canes should be removed and disposed of in the trash. A good autumn cleanup around your roses will help prevent spores from over-wintering on leaves and canes. Although beyond our control, cold, harsh winters and hot summers reduce the occurrence of rust as these conditions are not favourable to the disease.

Balling or Browning

DESCRIPTION: Balling is a condition caused by the common fungus *Botrytis* which causes rose petals to stick together. This condition is most often observed in cool moist springs. Balling seems to affect very double flowered roses with thin petals.

DAMAGE: Infected buds or blooms will not open properly. They will eventually turn brown or fuzzy grey and die without producing a bloom.

CONTROL: If balling is a problem in certain roses the best solution is to remove the offending bush and plant a rose whose blooms are not affected. However, if the problem is not too widespread, the affected buds can be forced open.

Crown Gall

DESCRIPTION: Crown gall appears as a lumpy growth around the base of a plant. Galls are caused by the bacterium *Agrobacterium tumefaciens*. The crown gall bacteria can live in the soil for several years and enters the plant through wounds near its base. Galls are green at first and become rougher and browner with age. As new gall tissue forms, the old galls rot and shed bacteria into the soil. On small plants and shrubs, the galls are usually 5 cm (2 in.) in diameter.

DAMAGE: Rose bushes can live for a long time with crown gall, but become weak as the gall interferes with the uptake of water and nutrients. The plant may die if the gall completely encircles the stem.

CONTROL: The best control of this disease is prevention as once galls are present on a rose, the only control is to remove the plant and as much of the soil around it as possible. Avoid damaging plants close to the soil, which would provide the bacteria with access to the plant. After pruning roses near gall infestations, sterilize your pruners or saw with a solution of 1 part bleach to 4 parts water. To avoid spreading the disease to new plants, check for galls before planting roses.

Dieback/Canker

DESCRIPTION: Dieback or canker is caused by a number of common fungi that infest a mature rose. The fungi will cause mature canes to turn black. Infestations may occur where a rose cane has not been pruned back to healthy green tissue.

DAMAGE: If left unchecked, dieback will progress down an infected cane from the tip to the base. The whole cane or sometimes the whole plant will die.

CONTROL: Prune and discard the infected canes. When pruning, cut 6 mm (¼ in.) above a healthy bud and do not leave stubs jutting above the targeted bud.

Fasciation

DESCRIPTION: Fasciation is caused by spontaneous cell mutation, the presence of certain pathogens, or damage to a growing tip of a rose. The affected cells multiply laterally, which results in fused stems or joined flowers.

DAMAGE: In most plants this condition is transient and will only affect a small portion of the rose.

CONTROL: If fasciation occurs, simply prune and discard the affected part of the rose.

Phyllody

DESCRIPTION: Phyllody occurs when plant hormones are out of balance. It results in a flower abnormality in which leaf-like structures replace flower organs. Normal hormone production can be disrupted by water stress, insect damage and infection by phytoplasmas and viruses. Phyllody in roses is likely caused by hot weather during the period of flower bud formation. Affected plants will usually have normal and abnormal flowers at the same time.

Floribunda roses are more likely to exhibit phyllody and this may be due to genetic susceptibility. The 'Green Rose', *Rosa chinensis viridiflora*, has a stable mutation causing phyllody in all its flowers.

DAMAGE: This condition does not affect the health of the rose.

CONTROL: To control, prune the infected flowers.

Proliferation

DESCRIPTION: Proliferation is not actually a disease. It occurs as apical cells multiply very quickly but do not stop dividing when a flower is produced. As a result, new rose blooms will produce rose buds at their centre. A large number of new buds within flowers may be produced. Proliferation affects certain rose cultivars more than others but can be seen in almost any rose. It is most often seen in spring.

DAMAGE: This condition does not affect the health of the rose.

CONTROL: To control proliferation, prune the affected flowers. The next flower produced by that stem should be normal.

II Growing Roses in Containers

ONE OF THE BEST AND EASIEST WAYS to grow roses in Calgary is to plant them in containers. Any type of rose can be grown in pots or planters although miniature roses are the most common. With suitable storage space for the winter, the potted roses can be enjoyed again the next spring.

Growing roses in containers provides a number of rewards. The first is that you can have splashes of colour and fragrance almost everywhere in the yard by scattering pots of roses. In smaller sized yards or those with lots of concrete, potted roses provide colour to areas which otherwise would be barren. A few strategically placed pots by patio doors or along the side of the driveway will soften and brighten the whole yard. Those who live in apartments or condos with only a balcony can have their own container rose garden. A potted rose with a pleasant fragrance sitting on the front step will have visitors sniffing with delight, especially if it is raised to an inviting level.

Another benefit is that potted roses can be moved around as desired. When a rose in a prominent place has finished blooming, it can be replaced by one that is blooming its heart out. Roses in pots can be moved to a more sheltered location (such as a garage or shed) if frost is forecast in early spring or late fall. This effort may be rewarded by an extra early or late flush of blooms, extending Calgary's short growing season. Miniature roses can be brought into the house when the weather turns cold.

Another advantage is in easy landscaping. A potted rose may be placed in a rose bed to test how its size and colours fit with the surroundings. If you like how it fits, the rose can be transplanted but if it is unsuitable, the pot can easily be moved. Roses in pots can also be used to fill in a bare spot in a perennial or annual bed as needed.

A rose in a pot can be placed anywhere in your garden with full sun, which means you can have more roses without sacrificing more grass and building more rose beds.

Selecting a Container

Planting the roses in an appropriate container is essential. The size and composition of the container are the most important considerations. Containers made of wood or unglazed ceramic are preferable to those of metal or plastic because they can "breathe" and will keep the roots cooler. However, plastic pots can be used if cost is a concern; they can be placed inside ceramic pots if desired. Whatever the type of pot, it must have large drainage holes in the base. If a pot does not have preformed holes, they can be created using an electric drill as punching holes often cracks the pot.

The container needs to be large enough to comfortably accommodate the rose's roots and should be in proportion to the size of the rose. Large, full grown roses will require larger pots. Roses that grow rapidly during the summer, such as climbers, will need larger pots than slow growing roses. However, keep in mind that Calgary's short summer means a rose will not reach its full size in one season and that any rose can be transplanted into a larger pot as it grows.

Sexy Rexy

Cinderella

One consideration is that roses in pots must be moved to a sheltered location during the winter. A lighter and smaller potted rose is more easily moved. However, smaller pots tend to dry out more quickly than larger ones and may have to be watered every day.

Most miniature roses will do well for several years in a 20 cm (8 in.) diameter pot, but they can be started in a 15 cm (6 in.) pot and transplanted. Patio roses or small shrub roses can be planted in a container 25 – 30 cm (10 – 12 in.) in diameter. Hybrid Teas, Floribundas and other large roses need containers at least 30 to 35 cm (12 – 14 in.) wide and deep.

Planting

Potted roses should be planted either in a commercial potting soil or a soil mix of 3 parts sandy loam soil to 1 part organic matter. Excellent organic additives are kelp meal, alfalfa pellets, compost and zeolite to hold water and nutrients. Water-retaining crystals can be used in smaller pots and those in hot, sunny locations. An inexpensive planting mix can be made by mixing 4 parts loam with 3 parts peat moss, 2 parts compost and 1 part perlite in a wheelbarrow or large container.

Before adding any soil mix to the container, rocks, broken crockery or heavy duty screen should be placed in the bottom of the pot. This will prevent the soil from washing out through the drainage holes after watering.

Add enough soil mix to the pot to form a mound and position the rose on top of the mound so that the crown is 3 – 5 cm (1 – 2 in.) below the rim of

Super Cascade Coral

the container. Holding the rose in position, fill the container with planting mix up to the crown. Press the soil down gently, then water thoroughly with a commercial transplant solution to lessen transplant shock. Do not fertilize at this time. The soil should eventually settle 3 – 5 cm (1 – 2 in.) below the rim of the pot, creating a reservoir to facilitate watering.

Location

Place potted roses in a sunny location where they will receive at least 6 hours of sun daily. The plants may survive in less sun, but they will not bloom as frequently or produce as many flowers.

In late July and August, the hottest part of the summer, pots in hot and exposed locations may need to be shielded or double potted to keep the roots cool and the plants healthy. This is less of a problem with wood or pottery containers, but roses in any type of container will benefit by being moved to where they are shaded during the hottest part of the day. Although there are roses that thrive next to light-coloured walls, do not place most containers in this environment. The excessive reflective heat and light will burn the foliage and dry out the blooms.

Watering

Roses in pots should be kept evenly moist. A thorough watering twice a week should suffice but you should monitor the moisture content regularly as a rose can change surprisingly quickly from appearing fine to being totally dry. In hot, dry weather, the roses will need to be watered every day.

Check the soil mix and if moisture is not felt 3 cm (1 in.) below the surface, water the rose.

Remember to check the soil moisture content of your pots even in rainy weather as the leaves of a large rose may prevent all but a little water from reaching the soil. A moderately sunny day can then cause the soil to dry out and the plant to wilt.

If the soil mix has a high peat content, it may shrink away from the sides of the container if it becomes too dry. It will then be difficult to rehydrate the soil as water will run down the inside of the pot and out the drainage holes rather than being absorbed. If this happens, the pot can be set in a bucket of water for a few hours to rehydrate the peat but do not leave the pot in water for too long as the rose will drown.

Fertilizing

Regular, frequent fertilizing is important as roses in containers deplete the available nutrient supply more quickly than roses in the ground. After the first flush of blooms appears, fertilize containers weekly

Margaret Merril

with a liquid plant food at half strength to prevent the accumulation of salts in the potting soil. It may be more efficient to fertilize a large number of pots once in the spring with a slow release fertilizer. The pellets should be worked into the soil around the base of the plant. Bare root roses should not be fertilized with chemical fertilizers the first year to prevent damage to the developing small feeder roots.

Winter Care

Roses grown in containers can survive temperatures of -2°C (28°F) without protection or covering so a spring or fall frost will not kill the roses. However, potted roses must be protected for the winter in Calgary's climate so they will grow again the next spring.

There are several methods that can be used to over-winter roses in containers in Calgary. These are discussed in more detail in the chapter *Winterizing Roses* but are summarized below.

Container roses can be overwintered in an unheated, insulated garage. The survival rate is better for large pots than small pots as they do not dry out as quickly. Cut the roses back to 20 – 30 cm

Flower Carpet Red

(8 – 12 in.) and place a collar around the rose. Fill the collar with peat moss and place the rose on a shelf for the winter. Water once every few months.

Potted hardy roses can be set into a garden bed in the fall. Winter protection can be provided with a couple of scoops of garden soil or mulch around the base of the plant. Place the pots in an area protected from the drying winter winds as the roses may otherwise dehydrate.

Potted tender roses can be buried in a large hole in the garden. Pots laid on their sides may deform from the weight of the soil piled on them, but they will straighten out in the summer. Wrapping the pots and plants in burlap or landscape fabric before burial will keep them cleaner. Do not wrap them in plastic as water can gather inside and drown the rose. Mouse poison placed in a short piece of PVC pipe and buried with the roses will help to control mice.

A large insulated box works very well for storing potted roses. Place large roses, such as climbers up to 2 m (7 ft.), into the box first, and stack smaller roses around them.

Smaller potted roses can be brought into the house and treated as houseplants for the winter.

Wind Rhythm

12 Rose Propagation

CREATING NEW ROSES IS AN EXCITING aspect of rose growing. Through propagation, more bushes of a particular rose can be started, or new roses can be created by cross-pollinating blooms from two different plants. Sometimes, however, it can be extremely difficult to propagate a rose while other times a piece of stem can be stuck in water and it will form roots.

For the rose enthusiast who would like to expand their rose collection, this chapter discusses three methods of propagating roses:

- stem cuttings;
- natural fertilization of rose seeds; and
- hybridization.

Before you start, keep in mind that propagating roses from certain registered cultivars is illegal without permission as royalties must be paid for each new plant. However, the primary purpose of this chapter is to describe propagation processes and we assume the end products will not be sold.

Stem Cuttings

Stem cuttings can be taken to create new plants of the parent rose by encouraging a small piece of cane cut from the parent to produce roots. One of the advantages of propagating roses from cuttings is that roses grown on their own roots are hardier and will not form suckers.

Two types of cuttings can be used to propagate roses: hardwood cuttings are taken from mature wood and softwood cuttings are taken from new growth. Softwood cuttings are easier to work with and will be discussed in detail here. It will take a full year to reproduce a rose from softwood cuttings.

Hybrid Tea roses are the most difficult to propagate using softwood cuttings. Old Garden roses, Floribundas, Miniatures, Shrubs and Species are much easier to propagate. Some miniature roses will form roots if you simply place cuttings in water in an opaque jar in indirect light. Experimentation will allow you to determine which roses are best propagated through softwood cuttings.

To reproduce roses by softwood cutting, you will need the following equipment:

- sharp knife, single-sided razor blades or sharp pruning shears;
- plastic pots (at least 15 cm or 6 in. in diameter);
- 2 litre (½ gal.) clear pop bottles with tops removed, or plastic bags with support stakes;
- sterile soil or soil-less mix;
- liquid or powdered rooting hormone; and
- grow light and bench.

Stem Cutting Process:

1. In June or early July, select the roses to be propagated. Inspect the canes for new growth and choose potential cuttings that are healthy and representative of the plant. It is best to take cuttings just after the bloom has finished.

2. Pots should be prepared immediately before obtaining cuttings. Match the pot size to the length of the cutting; longer cuttings will need bigger pots to support them. Put a small amount of slow-release fertilizer in the bottom of each pot and fill with soil mix. Water so the soil is moist but not soggy.

3. Label the pot with the cultivar name and the date the cutting was taken.

4. On the rose, select a stem that is 20 – 25 cm (8 – 10 in.) long with at least four or five 5-leaf sets attached. Remove the rose hip at the terminal end and any thorns; this may be more easily done once the cutting has been removed from the main plant.

5. Using a knife, make the lower cut just below the bottom 5-leaf set. Make an upper cut above the fifth 5-leaf set so that there are 4 or 5 sets of leaves on the cutting (see below). Remove the bottom set of leaves as this node is where the roots will form. The cutting can be placed in a tray of water to keep it from drying out if you are not going to pot it right away.

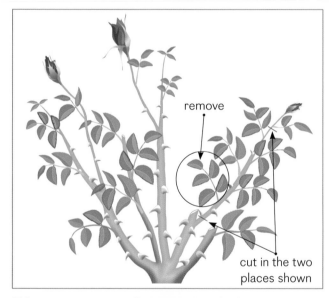

Taking a stem cutting. Cut cane as marked and remove the lowest of the 5-leaf sets as shown

6. The bottom 1 cm (½ in.) of the cutting should be dipped into a liquid or powdered rooting hormone. Make a small hole in the growing mix in the pot and gently tamp the cutting into place.

7. The high humidity necessary for the cutting to produce roots can be created by covering the pot with a plastic bottle or placing the pot inside a plastic bag. Use stakes to keep the bag away from the cutting. Set the pot by a window with bright, indirect light and keep the soil moist. If new growth is seen, the cutting has likely rooted.

8. Once rooted, the new roses should be "hardened off" by putting them outside for longer periods each day during the summer. Do not plant them outside.

9. Bring these roses back into the house in the fall as they will still be very tender. Place them under a grow light for the first winter. At the beginning of the second summer, if they have survived, the roses can be planted outside and enjoyed.

Natural Fertilization of Seeds

The natural fertilization method depends upon insects or wind to move pollen from a pollen parent to a seed parent to produce a fertilized hip. Under normal conditions, this hip will ripen in early fall and if left on the rose for the winter, it will release seeds the following spring which will grow into new roses. You can increase the odds of natural fertilization happening in your rose garden by planting some of the common pollen and seed parents, such as 'Hansa'.

In order to propagate new roses through natural fertilization, you need to harvest any fertilized hips and produce seedlings from them. These seedlings will produce a new rose but not all will be viable. And, because nature has done the breeding for you, you may not know which rose was the pollen donor. Propagating roses using this method will take about one and a half years.

To grow the roses produced by natural fertilization, you will need the following equipment:

- sharp knife or single-sided razor blades;
- clear jars;
- detergent and laundry bleach;
- towels;
- sealable plastic bags (Ziploc®);
- small plastic pots (15 cm or 6 in. in diameter);
- 2 litre (½ gal.) clear pop bottles with tops removed or plastic bags with support stakes;
- sterile soil or soil-less mix;
- liquid or powdered rooting hormone; and
- grow light and bench.

Natural Fertilization Process:

1. In early fall, any naturally fertilized hips will begin to ripen and turn pink, orange or yellow. Harvest the ripening hips when the colour first changes. If there is danger of a hard frost, cut off a length of the branch with the hip and place it indoors in a glass of water, giving it a little more time to ripen.

2. Cut the hip open with a sharp knife once it is ripe and dark in colour. Remove any seeds and place them in a water-filled jar to which a drop of detergent and a drop of laundry bleach have been added. Swirl the seeds around to wash them. Any seeds that float in clean water can be discarded as they are likely sterile. Finally, rinse the remaining seeds in clean water and allow them to dry on a towel.

Rose hip with ripe seeds

3. Place some of the soil mix in a small jar or sealable plastic bag and add enough water so the soil is moist. Add the seeds to the soil and mix. Label the jar or bag with the name of the rose from which the hip was harvested as well as the date and place it in a refrigerator at 4°C (39°F) for about 5 months.

4. Examine the jar or bag in February or March. If thread-like roots have appeared on the seeds, they are ready for planting. Plant each seedling in a small pot filled with the soil mix. Cover the seedlings with plastic bottles or enclose them in plastic bags to create a greenhouse climate.

Seedling produced from fertilized Hansa hip

5. Place the potted seedlings in bright, indirect light or under grow lights and keep the soil moist. In about 3 months, the seedlings should have some new growth with about 3 sets of leaves. If no new growth has appeared, the seedling is most likely dead and can be discarded.

6. The new roses should be "hardened off" by putting them outside for longer periods each day during the summer. Do not plant them outside.

7. Bring these roses back into the house in the fall as they will still be very tender. Place them under a grow light for the first winter. At the beginning of the second summer, if they have survived, the roses can be planted outside and enjoyed. Don't forget to give your rose a name, but make sure you record the seed parent.

Hybridization

Hybridization involves the pollination of a selected seed parent by a selected pollen parent in a controlled environment. This is the method that rose breeders use to create new roses. Essentially, the rose breeder takes the role that wind or insects play in the natural fertilization process. It is the most difficult and time consuming of the three methods described here, but it is still possible to propagate new roses in this manner using roses from your garden. It will take about two and a half years to produce a new rose through hybridization.

Some understanding of rose biology is necessary at this point. All roses are bisexual with both male organs (stamens) and female organs (pistils). The pistils, located at the bloom's centre, are delicate

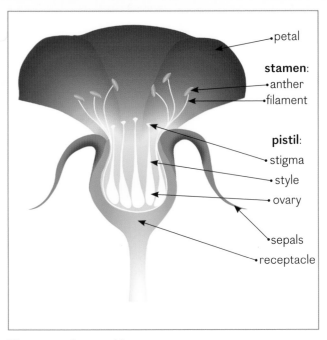

The parts of a rose blossom

stalks connected to an ovary at the bottom end with a pollen-receiving stigma at the tip. The stamens, slender filaments topped by anthers, surround the pistils and hold pollen.

The first step in hybridizing roses is to ensure that you have two potential parents growing in your garden or a garden you have access to. Both a pollen parent and a seed parent are required. Most roses can be used as a pollen parent, but only roses that set hips can be a seed parent. You can check your roses in the fall to find out which set hips and then use them for hybridizing the following year. An alternative is to plant commonly used seed parents in your garden. These can be determined by looking at the parentage of any rose. When the parentage is listed, the seed parent is always first, with the pollen parent last. So, in a cross of 'White Masterpiece' × 'First Prize', 'White Masterpiece' is the seed parent and 'First Prize' is the pollen parent. You can plant the seed parents that you like in your garden and then use them in your hybridization experiments.

To grow the seeds produced by hybridization, you will need the following equipment:

- sharp scissors or knife;
- tweezers;
- poly bag with labels and ties;
- small paintbrush;
- clear container with lid and label; and
- all equipment used in natural fertilization process.

Hybridization Process:

1. In spring or early summer, during the first flush of blooms on your selected seed parent, select a blossom that is about half open. This blossom must remain on the bush as you carefully remove all the petals either by hand or using tweezers. Remove all the anthers using small scissors; the filaments can remain without impairing the process. Place a poly bag over the hip to protect it from wind- and insect-borne pollen. Label it as the seed parent.

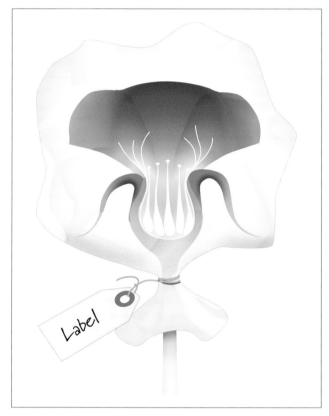

Covering the seed parent

2. Next, select a blossom from the pollen parent that is about half or more open. Remove the anthers with scissors and place them in a small clear container. Put the lid on the container and label it with the date and the name of the pollen parent. One to two days later, the anthers in the container will ripen and release dust-like pollen grains that contain sperm.

3. Monitor the stigmas on the covered seed parent closely. When the tips are covered in a sticky secretion, usually one to two days after preparation, it is time to pollinate. Remove the poly bag from the seed parent and use a small brush to apply the pollen from the lidded container to the stigmas. Both the pollen and the stigmas must be dry. Once the pollen has been brushed on, replace the bag over the seed parent. Record the pollen parent on the label.

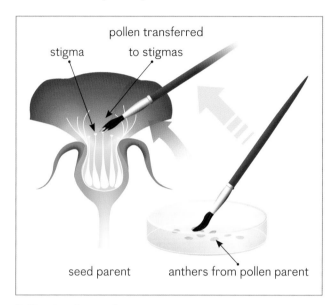

Pollinating the seed parent

4. Watch the seed parent hip for the next month. If it remains green and swells within 3 – 4 weeks, the rose is pregnant. However, if the hip dries up and falls off the plant, fertilization did not take place. The poly bag can be removed once the hip starts to swell, but ensure the label is not lost.

5. In the fall, 3 – 4 months after pollination, the fertilized hips will begin to ripen and turn colour. The steps described in the previous section *Natural Fertilization Process* should now be followed to produce a new rose bush.

🌹 🌹 🌹

A TALE OF TWO SUCKERS

Suckers from own-root roses are a good way to propagate the plant, particularly with shrub roses. If time is available, allow the sucker to grow for a year or two, and then sever the feeder root from the main plant. Let the sucker continue to grow for another year, until it will has developed enough of its own root system that it can be transplanted. If less time is available, simply digging up a sucker with a piece of root and transplanting it can work, but expect that it will not always be successful.

Some shrub and species roses sucker so vigorously that they can expand into unwanted areas and can become a nuisance. They do this by sending out strong lateral roots which can travel beneath the ground surface for up to a few metres before they send up a sucker. Shrub and species roses which are known to be prone to suckering are best contained by impermeable subsurface barriers.

Suckers from a low-growing hardy shrub rose advancing across a path.

A thicket of suckers surrounds the base of this hardy shrub rose.

Tender Hybrid Tea rose which has 2 stems growing from the bud union while there are several thin suckers growing to the side of the bud union.

Suckers from grafted roses originate from the hardy rootstock below the bud union. While not common, suckers will occasionally develop while the tender grafted rose is alive. The suckers can usually be identified because they are thinner and more willowy than the canes of the grafted rose. They may also be a different colour and may have different shaped leaves. These suckers can sometimes overwhelm the tender rose and kill it. Such suckers should be torn (not cut) from the roots and discarded. If the sucker is cut at ground level, or even below ground, it will continue to live and will regrow.

If a tender grafted rose winter kills, the hardy root may continue to live and will send up suckers. Experience shows that in Calgary, on a rose that has winter killed, suckers from the roots will appear around the end of June or first of July, providing false hope that the rose has just been slow in breaking dormancy. Check these late shoots carefully to find if they are coming from the bud union or from the roots.

Grafted roses in Canada are usually on Multiflora root stock. If the suckers from the roots are allowed to grow, they can develop into a huge bush that dies back each winter, and which blooms only after the mildest winters.

Grafted rose (dead)

Bud union

Shank

Suckers

Roots

The parts of a grafted rose with suckers.

Tear the suckers from the roots

Suckers should be torn from the roots so as to leave no parts to regrow.

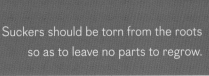

3.0 m (10 ft.)

Rosa Multiflora has grown from the rootstock after the grafted rose died. Canes grow more than 3 m (10 ft.) in one year but die back each winter.

13 The Rose Show

MANY PEOPLE GROW ROSES SIMPLY for their beauty and fragrance. Frequently, however, rosarians wish to share their roses' beauty in a more structured, competitive setting by exhibiting their blooms in a rose show. A rose show is more than a competition; it is an educational and social event with an opportunity to win ribbons and trophies. Through participation in the show, observation and discussion, gardeners learn how to select, grow, prepare and display roses.

The Calgary Rose Society believes that having a rose show encourages people to grow roses. Our annual Rose Show is held in late July or early August each year, timed to take advantage of the first flush of blooms on most tender roses.

Exhibiting at a rose show for the first time can seem like a daunting task. However, the process is simple and straightforward: determine what type of rose you have, what its official colour is, label it and place it on the table in the appropriate location. There are many others around to help make the process fun and easy. Prior to the show, the Calgary Rose Society holds a half-day "hands on" workshop to show how to select, prepare and display roses for the show. This is an informal session where you are free to ask questions and participate with your own experiences, problems and successes.

The Calgary Rose Show has many different categories or classes in which to enter your roses. Some are simple put-rose-in-container classes that can be prepared at the Show, while others include arrangements or corsages that need to be assembled ahead of time. There is something for everyone and both novice and experienced entrants are welcome!

Preparing Roses

Preparing your roses for the show doesn't have to be a last minute affair. Much can and should be done ahead of time as roses require time to grow and become show quality. You should start assessing your roses for potential show entries about 3 to 4 weeks before the show. Check the garden frequently for additional potential entries and groom them as necessary while still in the garden.

Disbudding

Classes for individual roses call for a single bloom on a strong, straight stem. To achieve this perfect form on potential entries, any side buds on the same stem as the main bud should be removed. Use a sharp knife or your fingers to remove the side buds. Once the disbudding is complete, the rose's energy will be directed towards the primary bud, which results in a larger bloom. Disbudding should be done two to four weeks prior to the show, otherwise it will be apparent and your entry may be penalized.

Unsymmetrical spray

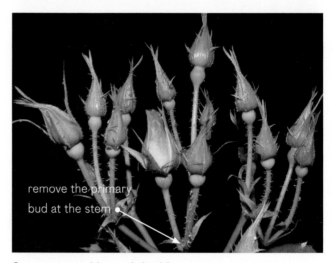

Spray primary bloom disbudding

Single bloom disbudding

Good entries in spray classes have uniform blooms over the entire spray. However, many sprays grow with a primary bloom emerging a few days before the bulk of the blooms. If left unchecked, this primary bloom will either dominate the spray or have finished blooming when the rest of the spray is in exhibition form. If you have a spray with either of these cases, it will not win an award.

To create a uniform spray, remove the largest bud at the point where it emerges from the stem, two to four weeks prior to the show. The side buds on the main stem will then develop and fill in the now

empty space. Removing the primary bud after it has finished blooming will probably result in penalties if the disbudding is apparent.

Bloom Protection

Pale coloured blooms can be damaged or spotted by rain. A few days to a week before the show, protect any potential entries by placing a plastic bag, a milk carton, an inverted Styrofoam cup or a plastic sheet on top of a stick over the bloom. Make sure the cover prevents the rain from touching the bloom but still allows the bloom to grow and develop.

Preserving Show Entries

Three to four days before the show, begin scouring your garden for potential entries. If a perfect show specimen is found, cut the bloom with as long a stem as possible. Place the rose in a water-filled container, with or without floral preservative. Refrigerate the rose until the day of the show to preserve the bloom, but do not place it in a refrigerator that contains fruit. Every fruit, especially apples, will release ethylene gas that could spoil your entry by forcing the bloom to open further. Cut entries can also be stored in a cool area of the basement or cellar until the day of the show. A bloom can be preserved exactly as cut for about four days, no longer.

The Day of the Show

Cutting Show Entries

Most exhibitors in Calgary cut their show roses either the day before or the morning of the show. Choose entries with single blooms that are half to three-quarters open. The roses should be cut either early in the morning or very late in the evening as roses cut during the middle of a hot day tend to wilt even if their stems are immediately placed in water. Early morning, just after sunrise, is best for cutting as they tend to survive longest. A good show entry should have a stem that is in proportion to the size of the bloom, so cut the stem as long as possible.

Attach a label to each potential show rose immediately after cutting, before placing it in a container. A tag or tape with the name of the rose should be affixed to the stem. Once indoors, re-cut the stem under water at a 45 degree angle, removing no more than 1 cm (½ in.). This prevents air bubbles from entering the stem which would hinder the flow of water to the bloom. The final stem cut and entry grooming can be done at the show.

Transportation

Once your entries have been selected and cut from the garden, they must be transported to the show location. There are a variety of methods for doing so. Glass jars, plastic bottles or even vases are good vessels for transportation, but may not be used for show display. Place the jars in a cardboard box or other large container and separate the jars with crumpled newspaper or towels to prevent possible breakage or water spillage. Whatever method you choose, ensure the rose stems are immersed in water and do not leave roses in the sun or in the car too long as the roses may wilt.

Arrival and Registration

Upon arrival at the venue, you must register with the Show Secretary to obtain an exhibitor number.

This number must be included with all entered roses. If assistance is required at any time, consult the Show Secretary, Show Manager or Show Chair, the organizers of the event.

It is better to arrive at the show early to ensure you have plenty of time to prepare your roses. A late arrival may result in there being little or no workspace for you and rushing through preparation may mean your roses are not at their best. If you cannot arrive early, limit your entries so that you have ample time to give each rose proper attention.

Preparation and Grooming

A grooming kit is helpful when preparing entries for exhibition. It should contain the following:

- soft clean cloths, paper towels or cotton swabs;
- Q-tips®;
- ballpoint pens or pencils;
- tweezers;
- small sharp scissors;
- small brush;
- rose cutters or pruners;
- wedging material (cork, Styrofoam, rhubarb); and
- sharp knife.

All display containers, including vases, bowls and English boxes are provided by the Society and must be used, except in the arrangement classes. This provides uniformity and allows the judges to concentrate on the roses, not the vessels in which they are displayed.

Collect as many of the supplied vases as needed, fill them with water, and floral preservative if you desire. Place one entry in a filled vase and, if necessary to produce a better presentation, position wedging material around the stem so that the rose is upright and centred in the container.

To maximise your rose's winning potential, groom it once it is positioned in the vase. The foliage can be cleaned with a soft, damp cloth but do not apply oil or ink as these substances can disqualify the entry. Use a brush to remove any fine dust or debris from the bloom petals. Brown or torn edges on petals or leaves can be discretely trimmed with scissors. Unwanted growth may be discretely removed and damaged guard petals can be removed by gently pulling them off. Be careful not to significantly alter the shape of the rose. Do not remove any leaves above the lip of the container as roses can be penalized for lack of foliage. Be sure the stem is submerged in the water so the rose does not wilt.

Check the proportion of the bloom to the stem. If the stem is too long, trim it to the appropriate size. Conversely, if the stem is too short, raise it up in the vase using wedges to achieve better proportion to the bloom. Make certain that the wedging material does not protrude above the top of the container, although a small protrusion will not be penalized during judging.

Roses with insects will be disqualified, so it is important to remove them prior to entering your rose. Insects can be removed by delicately brushing with a small brush or Q-tip or by lightly spraying the blooms with water. Another alternative is to gently submerse the whole stem and bloom in a pail of cool water. Leaves can be dried afterwards with a soft towel, knitted glove or an old sock.

Your rose should now be looking its best.

Entering Roses

The Annual Rose Show Schedule is the guidebook to entering roses in the Calgary Rose Show. It lists all the rules for participating in the show and also includes dates, entry times and judging times. The most important piece of information in the Schedule is the list of rose classes available for entry. A copy of the Schedule is usually included with the July/ August edition of the Rose Round-Up newsletter or it can be obtained by contacting the Rose Round-Up editor. The Show Schedule is also available for downloading on the Calgary Rose Society website <http://www.**calgaryrosesociety.ca**>.

The official entry tags supplied by the Society must be used to enter roses in the classes. These tags can be obtained from the Show Secretary upon registration. All portions must be completed. As this can be time consuming if you have a multitude of roses to enter, obtain some entry tags ahead of time and fill in the appropriate blanks before the show. Address labels or a rubber stamp may be used to enter your name. Write your exhibitor number on both the upper and lower portion of all entry tags. Don't forget to write the name of the rose on the tag and remove your transportation label.

The section and class that you are entering your rose into must also be written on the entry tag. To

Calgary Rose Society

Year: _____

Section: _____ Class: _____

Rose Name: _____

Exhibitor's No.: _____

Name: _____

Member: ☐ Yes ☐ No

Awards

1st	2nd	3rd	HM
☐	☐	☐	☐

----------------------------- *fold here* -----------------------------

Awards

☐	☐	☐	☐
1st	2nd	3rd	HM

Year: _____

Section: _____ Class: _____

Rose Name: _____

Exhibitor's No.: _____

Calgary Rose Show entry tag

determine the section, you must know what type of rose you have: Hybrid Tea, Floribunda, Grandiflora, Miniature, Climbing, Old Garden rose, English, Shrub or arrangement. The official colour must also be established as it will determine the entry class. A copy of the current Canadian Rose Society Colour Classification of Garden Roses handbook will be on hand at the show to confirm the type of rose and official colour. Then, consult the Annual Rose Show Schedule for the applicable section and class and record them on the entry tag. Place each of your entries in the appropriate class; the class sheets that accompany each class must be filled in with your exhibitor number and rose name.

Typical display tables at a previous Calgary Rose Show

Exhibitors may have as many entries as they desire in each class, but only one entry of each rose cultivar. If you have more than one example of a cultivar, choose the best example to enter in the class. All roses must be correctly named and classified. If you have a nice bloom, but cannot enter it in a particular class, consider entering it in an alternative class. If the rose cannot be entered at all, perhaps you could place it on the Rose Show Secretary's table so other people can enjoy it.

Clean Up

After entering your roses in the correct class, clean up the assembly area and return any unused vases. Vacate the staging area as soon as possible so that other entrants can prepare their exhibits.

All entrants must vacate the show by the time entry closes so that judging can commence. Once judging is completed and the show is re-opened the following day, you can check your results. The roses and ribbons remain on display all day for the public to enjoy. Trophies are presented at our Gala Evening in September.

Class Types

Rose Show categories include:

- Hybrid Tea single blooms and sprays;
- Floribunda single blooms and sprays;
- Grandiflora single blooms and sprays;
- Miniature single blooms and sprays;
- Climbing roses;

- Old Garden roses;
- English rose singles and sprays;
- Shrub rose singles and sprays;
- English boxes for Hybrid Teas and Miniatures;
- Arrangements (themed and bouquets);
- Corsages and boutonnieres;
- Rose in a Bowl; and
- Scented roses.

There are over 130 classes in which to enter your roses.

Explanations and examples of each type of class at the Rose Show are given below, as well as examples of some good and bad entries. If you are unsure about the suitability of one of your entries, either ask one of the Show Committee for advice or enter it anyway. While you might not win a ribbon for that rose, the judges' comments may include valuable advice for next year.

Judging entries at the 2009 Calgary Rose Show

Well formed spiral

High pointed centre

Confused centre

Outer petals too low

Single Bloom Roses

When viewed from above, a perfect single bloom rose will be ½ to ¾ open, with a well formed spiral centre. When viewed from the side, the bloom should have a high pointed centre with all petals above a horizontal line drawn at right angles to the stem and calyx tube. Two views of good entries in a single bloom category are shown with the red roses above.

When viewed from above, a single bloom rose should not have a faulty or confused centre. From the side, the outer row of petals should not fall below a horizontal line drawn at right angles to the stem and calyx tube. Two views of deficient single bloom roses are also shown with the yellow roses above.

Single bloom entries must be shown on one stem, with the exception of shrubs and Old Garden roses. Any blossom grown and displayed on a side stem (stem on stem) will be disqualified if the cut stem is apparent. To hide the cut, it can be placed within or below any wedging material so that the judges cannot see the stem on stem portion.

Spray Roses

A spray of roses entered in a spray category should have a regular outline without gaps or projecting blooms. The spray should have a uniformly rounded shape. A spray must include at least one flower that is three-quarters open and two buds which show colour.

stem on stem

Single bloom rose on a side stem

Winning spray entry

Rose in a Bowl

A rose exhibited in this class should have a classic single bloom shape and the bloom should be ½ to ¾ open, with a well formed spiral centre. The rose must be shown with its own foliage. The size of the bloom should be in proportion to the bowl. A rose bowl provided by the Society must be used.

Winning Rose in a Bowl entry

English Box

An English Box is a display of six Hybrid Tea or Miniature roses in a box supplied by the Society. Each individual rose should have the classic single bloom shape, but without foliage and placed so the stem can't be seen. All of the roses should be

similar in size, show symmetry and be displayed in a pleasing colour arrangement. Each rose must be named. English boxes are a good place to use blooms that have poor foliage or short stems because neither are required.

Winning Miniature English Box entry

Arrangements

There are two types of arrangement classes in the Calgary Rose Show. One type has themes that must be illustrated in some way by the arrangement. The second type comprises bouquets of roses placed in vases or baskets supplied by the exhibitor. Purchased flowers can be used in the themed arrangement classes; garden grown flowers must be used in the bouquet classes.

Trophy winning themed arrangement

Typical boutonniere entry

Full blown rose in the garden

Corsage and Boutonniere

Corsage and boutonniere classes provide an opportunity for personal design by the exhibitor, while conforming to the traditional corsage and boutonniere purpose. For the show purposes a corsage is defined as a small lightweight arrangement of flowers and foliage suitable for a lady's evening wear. It should be balanced and the proportions should be pleasing to the eye. A boutonniere is a small lightweight 'buttonhole' flower (rose), suitable for a gentleman. For both, roses must predominate and must be home grown.

Full Blown Rose

Entries in the full-blown rose class must have some stamens showing. The rose must be typical of the variety, but have opened wide to show the stamens within the bloom. The petals should have retained their freshness and colour without losing their substance or shape.

14 Favourite Hardy Roses

ONE OF THE PURPOSES OF THIS BOOK is to provide lists of roses that grow well in Calgary. This chapter lists 32 of the Calgary Rose Society's favourite hardy roses, chosen from over 100 suggested by rose society members. These top 32 roses were selected on the basis of performance and preference by members across the city.

For each of the favourite roses, we have included data on the rose's flower and bloom, fragrance, full growth size, foliage and recommended winter protection. The comments made by Calgarians growing the rose are also presented as well as background information. There is a photograph of every rose listed, taken of the rose in a Calgary area garden.

Although all of the roses described in this chapter will survive Calgary winters without protection, some may benefit from an application of mulch, and these are indicated. Most of the hardy roses will get some winter tip kill, some will die back to the ground, but all will recover and bloom the following summer.

Any one of these roses will make a colourful and beautiful addition to your garden.

Adelaide Hoodless

Parkland/Morden

FLOWER: Although the official colour of the flowers on 'Adelaide Hoodless' is deep pink, it really is medium red, and when it is in full bloom, it is a large red mound. Individual blooms are semi-double to double and medium sized. Blooming is continuous from early summer to frost.

FRAGRANCE: Light, if any.

FORM & FOLIAGE: A well branched, sun loving, easy care rose with glossy leaves. It will grow to about 1.5 m (5 ft.) in height and width. It has good disease resistance.

WINTER PROTECTION: None required. Any dieback will re-grow vigorously.

COMMENTS: "Blooms on new wood. The first flush end of June to early July with hundreds of blooms. Repeats well. Canes bend over when heavy with flowers." "Lovely colour. Very hardy." "One of the best hardies." "This rose seems to always be in bloom. Needs support." "Loves the sun and takes the wind well. My favourite shrub! It is drought tolerant, as are most of the Morden varieties. A very easy rose to grow."

Altaica

Rosa spinosissima

FLOWER: This rose has a 5 petal single flower that is white with a little pale yellow center. The bloom is about 8 cm (3 in.) in diameter. The bush is absolutely covered in flowers when it blooms. It gives one single flush in early June, and is one of the first flowering roses. The flush lasts two to three weeks with a few later blooms.

FRAGRANCE: None to minimal.

FORM & FOLIAGE: 'Altaica' is a huge bush that can grow to about 3 m (9 ft.) in height. The foliage remains nice all summer as it does not die or brown until late fall. The leaves are smaller in size than most other roses.

WINTER PROTECTION: None required.

COMMENTS: "Makes the neatest huge, dark red, almost black hips. Nice winter presentation of hips which stay on the bush." "This bush requires a large area. I have it planted in the alley and the yard. It is an absolutely gorgeous rose but it certainly can spread. Trim to shape after it flowers to perk it up and remove any straggly branches. It is so beautiful that I wish it would bloom all summer."

Blanc Double de Coubert

Hybrid Rugosa

FLOWER: The pure white double blooms of 'Blanc Double de Coubert' repeat well through the summer into the fall. The flowers are medium to large size, growing as singles and small clusters. The papery petals are easily damaged by rain.

FRAGRANCE: Strong, sweet and pervasive.

FORM & FOLIAGE: This rose has outstanding disease resistance. Plants grow to about 1.2 m (4 ft.) in height, with very thorny stems. Foliage is dark green, crinkled and in enough abundance to clothe the plant. However, sometimes the lower branches can be a little bare. It produces beautiful fall colouring and showy hips.

WINTER PROTECTION: None required. Very hardy.

COMMENTS: "May require extra Epsom Salts if leaves go yellow with chlorosis." "Low maintenance. Tough plant." "This rose is very disease resistant and very fragrant, but it does not bloom well in the shade. Best grown on its own roots, but is very slow to get established." "It suckers profusely."

Champlain

Explorer Shrub

FLOWER: 'Champlain' produces large numbers of small to medium sized, dark red, velvety looking blooms from early summer until fall. Cupped, double flowers, which look like Floribunda blooms, appear in small and large clusters all over the plant in a nearly continuous show. Regular deadheading will encourage even more blooms.

FRAGRANCE: Light.

FORM & FOLIAGE: Plants will grow to 1.2 m (4 ft.) in height and 1 m (3 ft.) in width. While the glossy foliage can occasionally get some powdery mildew, it is not a major problem. The plant has excellent resistance to black spot.

WINTER PROTECTION: None required. Minor winter tip kill.

COMMENTS: "Give it fertile soil, sun and water and it takes care of the rest." "Makes a beautiful show when grown in mass plantings or as a small hedge." "This is an easy rose to grow." 'Champlain' has won as best shrub in the Calgary Rose Show and received ribbons when used in a corsage and boutonniere.

Dunwich Rose

Rosa spinosissima

FLOWER: The 'Dunwich Rose' has small, single white flowers composed of 5 heart-shaped petals that lie flat so the yellow stamens project. These stamens give the rose a butter yellow center, like a poached egg. A once bloomer in early summer, it goes all out and covers itself with flowers. There may be a few late blossoms.

FRAGRANCE: Faint.

FORM & FOLIAGE: This is a low growing shrub up to 60 cm (2 ft.) in height, growing wider than it is tall. The tiny little leaves look like mouse ears. 'Dunwich Rose' loves the sun and is well behaved. The canes have small prickles.

WINTER PROTECTION: None required. Mulch crown until established.

COMMENTS: "I first fell in love with this rose in the UK, in David Austin's garden, where it was putting on such a stunning show that it completely took my breath away. I find it to be a very cheerful rose that I smile at every time I pass by. It has a few tiny hips in fall. I planted it in the most visible location in my garden."

Frühlingsgold

Spinosissima Hybrid

FLOWER: 'Frühlingsgold' is a once blooming shrub with a spectacular show of large, single, yellow blooms with dark yellow stamens. It is one of the first roses to bloom in the spring. Blooms are produced all along the arching canes from the previous year's growth.

FRAGRANCE: Moderate.

FORM & FOLIAGE: The foliage is medium green and healthy and the growth is as tall, arching canes. 'Frühlingsgold' produces large, black hips.

WINTER PROTECTION: None required once established. Protection recommended for the first two years.

COMMENTS: "'Frühlingsgold' takes a while to establish but is well worth the effort. Disease free."

Golden Wings

Modern Shrub

FLOWER: 'Golden Wings' has large, pale yellow, single flowers with reddish stamens, born singly and in clusters. The blooms look fragile, but withstand wind and rain very well.

FRAGRANCE: Light.

FORM & FOLIAGE: The bush is vigorous and prickly, with many twiggy stems and light green leaves. This rose grows about 60 cm (2 ft.) in height and 30 cm (1 ft.) in width.

WINTER PROTECTION: Minor protection required, mulch crown with peat moss or leaves.

COMMENTS: "Deadheading keeps the bush in flower. 'Golden Wings' has some winter die back but will re-grow well in the spring."

Hansa

Hybrid Rugosa

FLOWER: The blooms of 'Hansa' are classified as medium red, but they are really more of a mauve red or purple pink. There is a main flush of blooms in late spring and then more or less continuous bloom until stopped by frost in the fall. The blooms are floppy, double, medium to large in size and appear mostly in small clusters, with a few singles.

FRAGRANCE: Strong.

FORM & FOLIAGE: 'Hansa' grows into a thick, prickly bush up to 2 m (6 ft.) in height with healthy, medium green, matte, very rugose leaves. It is immune to black spot. The leaves will occasionally turn pale with chlorosis if the soil is lacking in iron.

WINTER PROTECTION: None required.

COMMENTS: "Wonderful perfume. Reminiscent of cloves." "Thrives on neglect. Do not spray." "Great at the back of a perennial border." "Prune to remove winterkill and to keep it from taking over the garden." "We know of a plant that has had no protection for 38 years."

Harison's Yellow

Hybrid Foetida

FLOWER: A deep yellow, once flowering shrub, 'Harison's Yellow' was introduced in 1830. The small, semi-double flowers are produced in clusters all over the plant. It makes a bright show for 2 or 3 weeks in June.

FRAGRANCE: Moderate to very fragrant.

FORM & FOLIAGE: The plant grows into a thick bush up to 1.5 m (5 ft.) in height and width with rich green, matte leaves. It is susceptible to black spot but otherwise is disease resistant. 'Harison's Yellow' thrives in poor soil or rich, dry climates or wet, hot areas or cold.

WINTER PROTECTION: None required.

COMMENTS: "Plant it and forget it, but come back to enjoy the bright yellow display for 2 weeks in June." The rose originated in the garden of George F. Harison, an attorney in New York City. Early American settlers took this rose with them as they crossed the country and it became known as the Yellow Rose of Texas.

Hazeldean

Shrub

FLOWER: 'Hazeldean' produces bright medium yellow blooms in great abundance for about three weeks in late June. The blooms are medium sized and semi-double, in small and large clusters. There is no repeat bloom.

FRAGRANCE: Moderate.

FORM & FOLIAGE: 'Hazeldean' suckers freely and grows into a dense thicket up to 1.5 m (5 ft.) in height. It is an easy rose to grow as it thrives on neglect. Disease resistance is good.

WINTER PROTECTION: None required.

COMMENTS: "Tough as old boots. Mine is in shade. Would bloom better in full sun." 'Hazeldean' was bred by Percy H. Wright, a plant hybridizer from Saskatchewan who specialized in producing hardy roses that could survive Canadian winters. If, in June, you see a bright yellow thicket of a rose on a boulevard, beside a gas station, or in an industrial area, it is almost certainly 'Hazeldean', its parent 'Harison's Yellow', or 'Persian Yellow'. 'Hazeldean' may be hard to find, but is still available in commerce.

Henry Kelsey

Explorer Shrub (Climber)

FLOWER: The flowers on 'Henry Kelsey' are a true medium red, without any pinkish tones. Flowering is prolific in a major flush in early summer, followed by sporadic bloom until frost in the fall. The blooms are medium sized, semi-double to double and open wide to show bright yellow stamens. Large clusters of blooms form at the ends of vertical canes, but along horizontal canes the lateral flowering nodes each produce a spray of blooms.

FRAGRANCE: Very little to mild.

FORM & FOLIAGE: The canes on 'Henry Kelsey' are long and lax. They can be tied to a trellis or fence to grow as a short climber, or left to sprawl as a wide, rather leggy shrub. Disease resistance is fair to good. Foliage is glossy and somewhat sparse.

WINTER PROTECTION: Hardy, but die back can be reduced by providing some protection.

COMMENTS: "To some people, the fragrance is spicy." "Be patient with this rose, it takes two or three years to establish." "This rose is truly red to me. I really like the colour contrast with the very bright yellow stamens." "If not deadheaded, it produces lovely red rose hips in the fall."

Hope for Humanity

Parkland/Morden

FLOWER: The cupped, semi-double to double flowers on 'Hope for Humanity' are among the darkest reds of any of the shrub roses. They are produced in small and large clusters in generous flushes throughout the summer.

FRAGRANCE: None to very faint.

FORM & FOLIAGE: The rose will usually grow to about 60 cm (2 ft.) in height and is a rather small, shy plant. However, one 'Hope for Humanity' in Calgary is 1.5 m (5 ft.) in height and blooms in flushes of at least 100 flowers. The plant blooms better in full sun. This is an easy rose to grow. Powdery mildew may be a problem.

WINTER PROTECTION: None required. Minor winter tip kill.

COMMENTS: "Plant holds blooms better than any other. A super shrub rose." "Love the colour of the blooms. Deep red at first, then lighter red when opened." "Very pleased with this rose." "It was named in honor of the 100th anniversary of the Canadian Red Cross."

J.P. Connell
Explorer Shrub

FLOWER: The medium yellow flowers of 'J.P. Connell' resemble Hybrid Teas when they first open. The medium-sized, double blooms then open wide and fade to a cream colour. In the hot sun they look almost white. The plant blooms in flushes through the summer. The colour of the blooms seems to get darker each year as the bush gets older.

FRAGRANCE: Faint.

FORM & FOLIAGE: 'J.P. Connell' has glossy foliage on thornless stems. It will grow to about 1 m (3 ft.) in height and 60 cm (2 ft.) in width. However, if it is covered for the winter to prevent die back, it can reach 1.2 m (4 ft.) in height. Like most yellow roses, it is susceptible to black spot. It has good resistance to powdery mildew.

WINTER PROTECTION: None required. Will die back each year.

COMMENTS: "I have grown this rose since it was first released and have five. It is a winner." "A faint tea rose scent." "Be patient with this rose. It takes 2 or 3 years to establish and then it will reward you." Although not truly an explorer, 'J. P. Connell' originated from the same breeding program in Ottawa.

John Cabot
Explorer Shrub (Climber)

FLOWER: The flowers produced by 'John Cabot' are classified as medium red, but appear as more of a deep pink or orchid pink. They appear in great clusters over a long blooming period in early summer and then repeat until fall. The blooms are medium sized, semi-double to double and open flat, but are often too crowded together to open fully. Blooms are produced over the entire plant.

FRAGRANCE: None to moderately strong.

FORM & FOLIAGE: This plant takes about 3 years to become established. In a protected sunny location with good soil and lots of water, 'John Cabot' will grow up to the eaves of the house and 1.2 to 1.8 m (4 to 6 ft.) in width. Prune to remove any winter kill and to keep the plant from escaping your garden. It is disease resistant, but leaf cutter bees love this rose.

WINTER PROTECTION: None required. Minor winter tip kill.

COMMENTS: "Grow it against a fence unless you do not mind staking. John is a very big boy!" "Very floriferous. Attracts a lot of attention." "A showy shrub in full bloom. Care free but looks better with deadheading." "This rose requires a lot of room to grow."

John Davis
Explorer Shrub (Climber)

FLOWER: Medium pink flowers grow in small and large clusters all over 'John Davis'. The blooms are double and medium sized, but loose and floppy in shape. However, the appeal is in the soft colour and the sheer mass of blooms. It is one of the longest blooming and most prolific of the shrub roses.

FRAGRANCE: Faint.

FORM & FOLIAGE: 'John Davis' will grow to 1.8 m (6 ft.) in height if given some support, but if not supported will grow wide and not as tall. New foliage is reddish and turns medium green as it matures. It gets a little black spot and mildew.

WINTER PROTECTION: None required. Minor winter tip kill.

COMMENTS: "Light spicy fragrance." "If you had to choose one explorer shrub, this one has it all." "Blooms in abundance." "A very healthy dependable plant." "Does not produce long canes until established (3rd year)." "This is my favourite Explorer rose." "My rose has gone through 2 winters and never had winter kill."

Morden Blush   *Parkland/Morden*

FLOWER: The official colour of 'Morden Blush' is light pink, but the blooms gradually fade to ivory. In a hot location, the blooms tend to be paler. The flowers are produced in small clusters all over the plant. Blooming is continuous from early summer until stopped by frost.

FRAGRANCE: Light.

FORM & FOLIAGE: This bushy little plant grows to about 1 m (3 ft.) in height and 60 cm (2 ft.) in width. The foliage is glossy and very disease resistant. 'Morden Blush' is a good plant for the novice rose grower.

WINTER PROTECTION: None required.

COMMENTS: "Beautiful blooms like small Old Garden roses. Colour fades over time." "A real beauty if given enough light. Likes the east sun. Tolerates the wind. Delicate looking." "Love the colour of the blooms. We have moved ours and it is doing better. I think that it likes a lot of sun." "Great rose. Flowers from June to September. I would always have one of these roses in my garden." "Dependable. Slows down in midsummer, but rarely out of bloom all through gardening season." "Quick to re-bloom."

Morden Snowbeauty   *Parkland/Morden*

FLOWER: The only white among the Parkland series of roses, 'Morden Snowbeauty' has medium sized, semi-double flowers that open flat to show golden yellow stamens. It blooms in small clusters with prolific flushes throughout the summer. Rain will cause the blooms to spot. 'Morden Snowbeauty' will flower all along the canes if allowed to lean.

FRAGRANCE: Light.

FORM & FOLIAGE: The plant is well clothed with glossy, disease resistant leaves. It will grow to about 1 m (3 ft.) in height and 75 cm (2.5 ft.) in width.

WINTER PROTECTION: None required.

COMMENTS: In September 1998, the Montréal Botanical Garden (Le Jardin Botanique de Montréal) carried out a survey of its well-established roses' resistance to black spot, powdery mildew and rust. This is one of the outstanding varieties that showed an infection rate of only 0 – 5%

Morden Sunrise   *Parkland/Morden*

FLOWER: The blooms of 'Morden Sunrise' are classified as yellow blend, but each flower contains shades of pink, cream and apricot. They are produced in small clusters all over the plant. The cupped blooms are single to semi-double and open wide to be almost flat.

FRAGRANCE: None to very faint.

FORM & FOLIAGE: This rose will grow to about 1 m (3 ft.) in height and 60 cm (2 ft.) in width with the bloom clusters at the top of the stems. The foliage is glossy and abundant. 'Morden Sunrise' likes lots of sun. It is a very healthy plant that is somewhat susceptible to black spot later in the season. This is an easy rose to grow for novice rose growers.

WINTER PROTECTION: None required.

COMMENTS: "Love the colour of the blooms." "Very good rose. Beautiful colouring. My second choice for hardy roses." "Visitors always want a closer look at this rose. Gorgeous."

Pink Grootendorst

Hybrid Rugosa

FLOWER: The small, unique blooms on 'Pink Grootendorst' are medium pink, double and fringed like the petals on carnations or dianthus. They are produced in small and large clusters in flushes all summer.

FRAGRANCE: None to faint.

FORM & FOLIAGE: The foliage has the typical wrinkled leaves of the rugosas with very prickly stems. The overall appearance of 'Pink Grootendorst' is a gaunt and prickly shrub with charming little flowers. It will grow in full sun or partial shade, but will bloom better in the sun. Aphids love this plant but it is remarkably free of disease.

WINTER PROTECTION: None required.

COMMENTS: "Pink carnation looking. Tough as old boots." 'Pink Grootendorst' is a sport of the medium red 'F. J. Grootendorst'. There is also a deep red sport 'Grootendorst Supreme'. 'Pink Grootendorst' has produced its own sport 'White Grootendorst'.

The Polar Star (Polstjarnan, Polestar, White Star or White Rose of Finland, The Wasa Star, Wasastiernan)

Hardy Climber

FLOWER: Small, single white blooms in open clusters appear all over 'The Polar Star' for about 3 weeks in early summer.

FRAGRANCE: None to faint.

FORM & FOLIAGE: The slender branches of 'The Polar Star' will climb up to 4.5 m (15 ft.) if they have something to support them. Its disease resistance is outstanding. It is an easy rose to grow but a challenge to contain. Deer will not touch it as it is too thorny.

WINTER PROTECTION: None required.

COMMENTS: "Very thorny." "Prune it to shape if you dare. Not grown so much for the individual blossoms as for the visual effect of entire shrub in full bloom. For that reason, it is good to give some thought to background and surroundings. My plant sort of disappears into my white fence." "It is a good choice for concealing unsightly objects." This is the most cold hardy climbing rose in the world.

Robusta

Hybrid Rugosa

FLOWER: 'Robusta' is a spectacular, eye-catching rose that produces scarlet red, single flowers up to 10 cm (4 in.) in diameter with yellow stamens. The blooms stay on the bush a long time. This is a repeat blooming shrub.

FRAGRANCE: Faint.

FORM & FOLIAGE: 'Robusta' can grow branches 1.8 m (6 ft.) in height but typically is about 1.2 m (4 ft.) tall. It has shiny, glossy leaves with large thorns as is typical of a rugosa. It is a very healthy rose that is not susceptible to disease.

WINTER PROTECTION: None required. Mulch crown until established.

COMMENTS: "This rose lives up to its name. Even though it may die back in winter, early in spring it starts constructing huge, thick, tall canes." "When people see the flowers on 'Robusta', they invariably ask, "What is that rose"? It is absolutely stunning and I've simply got to have one." 'Robusta' was bred by Kordes in 1979 and it seems to like the Calgary climate.

Rosa Acicularis

Species

FLOWER: 'Rosa Acicularis' produces light to medium pink, 2.5 to 5 cm (1 to 2 in.) blooms in small clusters. It blooms once in June to early July.

FRAGRANCE: Moderate.

FORM & FOLIAGE: This rose grows as a mounding bush 1 to 1.5 m (3 to 5 ft.) in height with very prickly canes. The older canes are dark red to brown. 'Rose Acicularis' has medium green foliage.

WINTER PROTECTION: None required.

COMMENTS: "Sweet fragrance." "Suckers vigorously, plant with a barrier to control where it can spread. The plant produces small, orange, red hips that persist through the winter. It displays beautiful red fall colour." Rosa Acicularis is the Alberta Wild Rose that blooms along fence lines and in woods each year in June.

Rosa Eglanteria

Species

FLOWER: 'Rosa Eglanteria' produces cherry pink blooms 4 cm (1.5 in.) in diameter each spring.

FRAGRANCE: Strong.

FORM & FOLIAGE: This rose grows strong, arching canes 1.2 to 1.5 m (4 to 5 ft.) in length and is slow to spread. The foliage is dark green and shiny. It is a healthy, disease free plant.

WINTER PROTECTION: None required. Mulch crown until established.

COMMENTS: "Very pretty ovoid red hips persisting through winter. Attractive shrub."

Rosa Forrestiana

Species

FLOWER: 'Rosa Forrestiana' is a deep rose colour, with blooms 2.5 cm (1 in.) in diameter that occur along the length of the cane. It blooms once in spring.

FRAGRANCE: Strong.

FORM & FOLIAGE: 'Rosa Forrestiana' has tiny mouse ear shaped, dark green leaves. It is a somewhat lax shrub, graceful and gorgeous in full bloom. It will grow to over 1.5 m (5 ft.) in height and width.

WINTER PROTECTION: None required. Mulch crown until established or if in exposed location.

COMMENTS: "Very attractive, graceful shrub. Slow to spread. Will produce hips once established."

Rosa Pendulina

Species

FLOWER: 'Rosa Pendulina' has single, bright cerise blooms that are 2.5 to 5 cm (1 to 2 in.) in diameter. It only blooms in spring.

FRAGRANCE: Very strong.

FORM & FOLIAGE: This bush grows to 2 m (6 ft.) in height and is a non suckering, upright shrub. It has medium green, healthy, generally disease free foliage. It may occasionally suffer from rust.

WINTER PROTECTION: None required. Mulch crown until established.

COMMENTS: "Attractive pendulous hips in the fall. Very pretty shrub in full bloom."

Rosa Pomifera (Villosa)

Species

FLOWER: 'Rosa Pomifera' has five cm (2 in.), soft pink, single blooms that are lovely against the bluish foliage. It is a one time spring blooming rose.

FRAGRANCE: Strong.

FORM & FOLIAGE: This is a large mounding shrub with blue green matte foliage. 'Rosa Pomifera' is non suckering and grows to about 1.2 to 1.5 m (4 to 5 ft.) in height.

WINTER PROTECTION: None required. Mulch crown until established.

COMMENTS: "Beautiful bluish foliage with unusual cherry red bristly hips. Very attractive in the fall." "Cool bluish leaves make a pretty background plant. Flowers are a soft pink and larger than most species roses and the plant doesn't sucker."

Rosa Primula (the Incense rose)

Species

FLOWER: 'Rosa Primula' has single soft yellow blooms that grow to 2.5 to 4 cm (1 to 1.5 in.). It blooms once in spring.

FRAGRANCE: Slight.

FORM & FOLIAGE: This rose has red brown stems and large translucent prickles with lacy looking dark green mouse ear shaped leaves. It is a tall plant, 2 m (6 ft.) in height with arching canes and is non suckering.

WINTER PROTECTION: None required. Mulch crown until established.

COMMENTS: "Gorgeous in full bloom. Foliage smells of incense when rubbed. Hips are purple-black, but do not stay on the shrub through the winter. Very attractive combination of cane colour and lacy foliage."

Schneezwerg
Hybrid Rugosa

FLOWER: 'Schneezwerg' has small, white, semi-double blossoms with yellow stamens in clusters of 3 to 10. Usually only 2 or 3 blooms are open at a time in each cluster, so that a cluster will gradually flower over a couple of weeks. The plant flowers continuously from June until frost with the largest flushes in the early summer and early fall. Early blooms will set hips while the plant continues to bloom, creating a very attractive display of white blooms and orange to bright red hips.

FRAGRANCE: Moderate.

FORM & FOLIAGE: 'Schneezwerg' has completely healthy, glossy, rugosa foliage which turns yellow and red in the fall. The dense, prickly shrub grows to 1.3 m (4.5 ft.) in height.

WINTER PROTECTION: None required. Minor winter tip kill.

COMMENTS: "Disease free. This is an attractive garden shrub. Rose curculios really like the blooms of 'Schneezwerg' and can spoil many blooms during the early summer flush."

Stanwell Perpetual
Pimpinellifolia (Spinosissima)

FLOWER: The blooms of 'Stanwell Perpetual' are classified as white, but they usually start out blush pink and then fade to white. The blooming is not quite continuous, but rather in a sequence of flushes all summer and into the fall. The flowers are medium sized, double and open flat and quartered with a pretty arrangement of quilled petals.

FRAGRANCE: Moderate.

FORM & FOLIAGE: The foliage is grey green on this very disease resistant shrub. It will grow to about 1 m (3 ft.) in height and width. The stems carry a multitude of prickles.

WINTER PROTECTION: None required. May die back each year.

COMMENTS: "Dependable plant." "I really like this rose. It used to do very well for me in full sun, but since I have moved it to the shade it doesn't bloom very much."

Thérèse Bugnet
Hybrid Rugosa

FLOWER: Medium pink blooms which gradually fade to light pink are produced nearly continuously from early summer until frost. Each ruffled flower is double with about 36 wavy soft-textured petals. The flowers are good for cutting since there are no prickles on the flower stalks. Blooms occur both as singles and small clusters.

FRAGRANCE: Very strong.

FORM & FOLIAGE: 'Thérèse Bugnet' is a thick, upright shrub 1.2 m (4 ft.) in height and width with vigorous growth. Abundant prickles develop on second year wood, but the new growth and flower stalks have no prickles. It has excellent disease resistance.

WINTER PROTECTION: None required.

COMMENTS: "This rose belongs in every Alberta garden. It has an Old Garden rose fragrance and flower shape. It will tolerate some shade, but does much better in full sun. It also has very pretty red canes for winter contrast. Excellent fall colour." This rose has won the Most Fragrant Rose trophy at the Calgary Rose Show. It was bred by Georges Bugnet of Legal, Alberta to withstand Alberta winters without protection.

Wasagaming

Hybrid Rugosa

FLOWER: 'Wasagaming' produces large, mauve pink, double flowers. It usually blooms only once, but occasionally will produce a few blooms later in the season.

FRAGRANCE: Very strong.

FORM & FOLIAGE: The growth is vigorous and arching with medium green rugosa foliage. The fall foliage is spectacular in yellow, reds and purples.

WINTER PROTECTION: None required.

COMMENTS: "Disease free." 'Wasagaming' was bred by Dr. Frank Skinner in Manitoba to survive Canadian winters without protection.

Winnipeg Parks

Parkland/Morden

FLOWER: Officially the blooms are deep pink and when a bed of 'Winnipeg Parks' is in bloom, there is abundant colour. This low spreading plant blooms continuously from early summer until frost. Individual flowers are medium sized, semi-double and cupped, with yellow stamens and come singly or in small clusters.

FRAGRANCE: Very slight.

FORM & FOLIAGE: 'Winnipeg Parks' grows up to 1 m (3 ft.) in height, but is often shorter, particularly when used as a landscape rose in poor soil and little care. The semi-glossy leaves have a reddish tinge when young. Its disease resistance is very good, especially to mildew.

WINTER PROTECTION: None required.

COMMENTS: "A real beauty. In bud form it looks like a Tea rose. Another hardy Morden variety that makes itself at home in the Calgary climate." "Needs little pruning. A low maintenance rose." "Classic rose shape. Small but nice." "My first choice for hardy roses." 'Winnipeg Parks' was bred in Manitoba to handle Canadian winters.

HARDY ROSE CHECKLIST: PERSONAL FAVOURITES

15 *Favourite Tender Roses*

THIS CHAPTER LISTS 81 OF THE Calgary Rose Society's favourite tender roses, chosen from 290 suggested by rose society members. These top 81 roses were selected on the basis of performance and preference by members from across the city. All of the roses described in this chapter are tender or semi-hardy and will not survive Calgary winters without protection. Roses which bloom on old wood that may survive the winter without protection but will not produce blossoms the next summer are also included.

In order to provide you with as much information as possible about these tender roses, we've included data on the rose's flower and bloom, fragrance, full growth size, foliage and winter protection recommended. The comments made by Calgarians growing the rose are also presented as are some noteworthy details. There is a photograph of every rose listed, taken of the rose in a Calgary area garden.

We have indicated which of these favourite roses is easy or hard to grow in Calgary. Roses that are easy to grow will easily survive winter with normal protection; those that are hard to grow require extra winter protection and even then, may experience severe dieback or even complete winterkill in harsh winters. We have included these roses because members love them and are willing to put up with a bit of fussing to have them in the garden. Roses that are average growers in Calgary may experience some dieback even with normal winter protection, but will most likely recover completely and bloom as normal during the summer. Detailed information on how to winterize roses is presented in the chapter on *Winterizing Roses*.

Tender roses require a little more effort to keep in the garden but will reward you with their beauty and fragrance!

Tender Roses

Alba Meidiland
Shrub

FLOWER: 'Alba Meidiland' produces large clusters of small white blooms in flushes. Each bloom is small, but it is the massed effect that is so attractive.

FRAGRANCE: None.

FORM & FOLIAGE: It is a low, spreading, ground cover rose that puts on a nice show and is very disease resistant. 'Alba Meidiland' grows to about 60 cm (2 ft.) in height and a little wider.

WINTER PROTECTION: Semi-hardy. Some winter protection required. Easy rose to grow.

COMMENTS: "A real performer." "Hardy on a south side foundation. Blooms nonstop from June to October." "When I think of it, I will go into the garden the evening before the first killing frost and rescue a bouquet of 'Alba Meidiland'." 'Pink Meidiland' is another Meidiland series shrub which grows to 1 m (3 ft.) with single, deep pink blooms with a white center. It is semi-hardy, easy to grow and very disease resistant. 'White Meidiland' is similar to 'Alba Meidiland', but with larger blooms.

Alba Semi-plena
Alba

FLOWER: This white Old Garden rose has medium sized, single to semi-double blooms in small clusters, produced once a year in early summer. It blooms on old wood. Tolerant of some shade, it will produce more flowers in full sun. Rain can cause spots on the petals.

FRAGRANCE: Strong.

FORM & FOLIAGE: A tall leggy plant, 1.5 m (5 ft.) in height, 'Alba Semi-plena' produces leaves and blooms near the top of thorny stems. It will bloom all along the stem if the stems are trained sideways. Strong new stems are produced from the base of the plant. Disease resistance is very good. Pruning is needed only to remove winterkill and old canes.

WINTER PROTECTION: Some winter protection required. Canes should be covered. Average rose to grow.

COMMENTS: "Sweet and strong fragrance." "Beautiful on a trellis or fence. White blooms with prominent yellow stamens and beautiful red orange hips in the fall." "Very thorny." 'Alba Semi-plena' was probably the White Rose of York in the Wars of the Roses in 15th century England. It is still used to produce attar of roses in Bulgaria.

Angel Face
Floribunda

FLOWER: 'Angel Face' produces an abundance of medium sized, mauve flowers with yellow stamens that open from fat buds. Each petal of the bloom has a wavy edge. Flowering is in 2 to 3 flushes per summer, but in a healthy, mature plant the flushes last so long that the plant is nearly always in bloom, although with only a few blooms at a time. Blooms are usually in small clusters.

FRAGRANCE: Moderate.

FORM & FOLIAGE: 'Angel Face' likes sun but will bloom in partially shaded areas. Its growth is rather leggy and sprawling, up to a height of about 75 cm (2.5 ft.). The leaves are large and glossy, but prone to both black spot and powdery mildew.

WINTER PROTECTION: Full protection required. Average rose to grow.

COMMENTS: "Well worth sniffing." "Despite the fussing that I have to do with this plant to control disease, it retains its place in my garden because of the abundance of fragrant blooms. I sniff them every time I pass."

Apothecary's Rose (R. gallica officinalis) *Gallica*

FLOWER: The deep pink, semi-double blooms appear in small clusters only once per year for an extended bloom period in mid summer. The blooms are very large and can appear more crimson than pink. It blooms on the previous year's canes.

FRAGRANCE: Strong.

FORM & FOLIAGE: The plant grows upright, compact and bushy, to about 1.2 m (4 ft.) in height and width. It has excellent resistance to black spot, but can get a little powdery mildew. It suckers but not aggressively.

WINTER PROTECTION: Semi-hardy. Requires some winter protection. Canes should be covered. Average rose to grow.

COMMENTS: "Sweet fragrance." "Protect the old canes over winter. Cleanup is more work, but it repays the effort." The 'Apothecary's Rose' is possibly the oldest rose to be cultivated in Europe. It served as the basis for a thirteenth-century perfume industry in the town of Provins near Paris and was used for medicinal purposes during the Middle Ages. It was the Red Rose of Lancaster in the Wars of the Roses in 15th century England.

Apricot Nectar *Floribunda*

FLOWER: 'Apricot Nectar' produces medium sized, cupped flowers of a beautiful, peach or apricot colour in flushes throughout the summer. The official colour is apricot blend. The double blooms are very large for such a small plant. This rose loves the sun.

FRAGRANCE: Very strong.

FORM & FOLIAGE: Plants are quite small, growing to about 60 cm (2 ft.) in height and width. When grown in full sun, the glossy foliage of this tough little rose is rarely bothered by disease or insects.

WINTER PROTECTION: Full protection required. Average rose to grow.

COMMENTS: "Fruity fragrance." "'Apricot Nectar' provides a spot of colour in the garden. Plant this rose where you can enjoy its fragrance." "One of my first Floribundas, this rose lured me into the Floribunda world."

Barbra Streisand *Hybrid Tea*

FLOWER: The blooms of 'Barbra Streisand' are large, mauve to lavender with a classic high centre. This rose produces abundant flushes of single blooms and small clusters on straight sturdy stems. The flowers have good substance and are wonderful for cutting and long lasting in the vase.

FRAGRANCE: Very strong.

FORM & FOLIAGE: 'Barbra Streisand' is well-branched, upright with strong stems and has abundant glossy foliage. It is strong and vigorous and grows to 1 m (3 ft.). Black spot can be a problem.

WINTER PROTECTION: Full protection required. Average rose to grow.

COMMENTS: "Wonderful fragrance." "Wonderful shape, fine for exhibition but blooms best in July." "Flowers retain their colour and are long lasting." "Clusters are usually long stemmed enough to cut short single blooms from the cluster. We love this rose. One of my wife's favourites. Provides lots of fragrant blooms to give away. Prolific bloomer. Three abundant flushes per summer."

Belami
Hybrid Tea

FLOWER: 'Belami' produces large, classic high center, pink blend blooms in singles and small clusters continuously on a prolific plant. The blooms do spot in the rain.

FRAGRANCE: Very strong.

FORM & FOLIAGE: 'Belami' thrives in full sun and grows to about 1 m (3 ft.) in height by 75 cm (2.5 ft.) in width. It is relatively disease free. The foliage is glossy, dark green with a leathery texture.

WINTER PROTECTION: Full protection required. Average rose to grow.

COMMENTS: "I love this rose for its constant and prolific bloom production. The blooms last well on the plant or in the vase. The fragrance will fill whole rooms. One of the few you can smell in the garden without getting close."

Big Purple (Stephens' Big Purple)
Hybrid Tea

FLOWER: This rose has large, dark mauve to purple pink blooms with a classic high center. The plant repeats with moderate bloom production of singles and small clusters. The blooms will spot in the rain.

FRAGRANCE: Very strong.

FORM & FOLIAGE: 'Big Purple' is a tall, upright plant, 1.2 m (4 ft.) in height and 75 cm (2.5 ft.) in width, which likes lots of sun. The foliage is matte green.

WINTER PROTECTION: Full protection required. Average rose to grow.

COMMENTS: "Outstanding colour and wonderfully fragrant, great for cutting. Very strong plants." 'Big Purple' won Queen of the Show at the 2009 Calgary Rose Show.

Bonica (Bonica 82)
Shrub

FLOWER: A single plant of 'Bonica' has been known to produce over 75 blooms at once. Each bloom is small, double and light to medium pink. The plant blooms in flushes with quick repeat, so that it seems to be nearly always in bloom.

FRAGRANCE: None to slight.

FORM & FOLIAGE: This rose is a rounded plant growing up to 1.2 m (4 ft.) in height that responds well to hard pruning. The foliage is glossy and very disease resistant. It likes all the sun it can get. Occasionally, it will get some black spot later in the season.

WINTER PROTECTION: Semi-hardy. Some winter protection required. Easy rose to grow.

COMMENTS: "I love this rose! Tons of flowers." "A real winner." In a survey undertaken by the Canadian Rose Society of rosarians across Canada, 'Bonica' was voted as the number one favourite shrub rose.

Brass Band

Floribunda

FLOWER: 'Brass Band' has very distinctive blooms with ruffled edges. While they are officially classified as apricot blend, most of the blooms are 2 or 3 toned blends of yellow, apricot, peach, pink and orange. This heavy blooming plant produces a few single blooms, but mostly sprays, both small and large, in flushes throughout the summer. The flowers tend to fade with time.

FRAGRANCE: None to faint.

FORM & FOLIAGE: The foliage is semi-glossy, dark green and very healthy. The upright and bushy plants will grow to about 1 m (3 ft.) in height by 75 cm (2.5 ft.) in width. This plant blooms best when grown in full sun.

WINTER PROTECTION: Full protection required. Difficult rose to grow.

COMMENTS: "Great rose. Very floriferous. Beautiful colour." "Consistent performer." "Brass Band can be difficult to get through the winter. I like this rose so much that I will buy a replacement 'Brass Band' each spring if I can find it."

Chapeau de Napoléon (Crested Moss, Cristata)

Moss Rose

FLOWER: 'Chapeau de Napoléon' has very double, deep pink blooms that fade to a silvery pink. It is a one-time bloomer with 4 cm (1.5 in.) flowers. The bloom period is about 45 days.

FRAGRANCE: Strong.

FORM & FOLIAGE: This is a very healthy, vigorous rose that is not aggressive. It grows to about 1 m (3 ft.) in height and width. It is not a true Moss rose because it only has moss-like growth below the blossoms. The sepals have stiff, branching edges that are pushed together into three ridges, resembling a cocked hat.

WINTER PROTECTION: Full protection required. Average rose to grow.

COMMENTS: "Has that heavy yummy old rose scent." "A word of warning: this rose breeds trespassers. Once they really look at it and see the neat little furry, green, tricorne hats under the blossoms, you just can't keep people away. Several times, there were two or three people standing in my yard, pointing and laughing at poor 'Chapeau de Napoléon' while he was blooming. Sets no hips." This is an Old Garden rose, bred in 1826. It was loved by Victorians for both its scent and soft, thick moss and was a symbol of love.

Cherry Parfait

Grandiflora

FLOWER: The large open sprays of blooms of 'Cherry Parfait' certainly get attention in the garden. While there may be debate about whether the red and white blooms are beautiful or garish, all can agree that they are very colourful. Each large, cupped, double bloom is held on a short stem off the main stem. The distribution of the red and white colours is different in each flower.

FRAGRANCE: Slight.

FORM & FOLIAGE: The large, sun loving plants can grow to 1 m (3 ft.) in height by 75 cm (2.5 ft.) in width and are very disease resistant.

WINTER PROTECTION: Needs full protection. Easy rose to grow.

COMMENTS: "Flowers last a long time. Very beautiful sprays." "Very showy." "Lucious colour. Yummy rose." 'Cherry Parfait' has won King of the Show three times at the Calgary Rose Show.

Chrysler Imperial
Hybrid Tea

FLOWER: 'Chrysler Imperial' produces large, classic high center, dark red double blooms in distinct flushes throughout the summer. The blooms are almost always produced one to a stem. Flower production is excellent, but it does tend to decline as the plant gets older. The blooms tend to age to a less pleasant maroon colour.

FRAGRANCE: Strong.

FORM & FOLIAGE: 'Chrysler Imperial' is smaller than some Hybrid Teas, reaching only 60 to 75 cm (2 to 2.5 ft.) in height and 45 to 60 cm (1.5 to 2 ft.) in width. Its foliage is matte green and prone to powdery mildew that deforms the leaves.

WINTER PROTECTION: Full protection required. Easy rose to grow.

COMMENTS: "Outstanding, marvelous fragrance." "Beautiful classic shape. Some blooms have muddled centers. If it had better disease resistance, it would be close to my ideal for a Hybrid Tea." "'Chrysler Imperial' has been around for a long time and some people will argue that there are newer red roses that are better, but it will always have a place in my garden." "An old faithful."

Day Breaker
Floribunda

FLOWER: Medium sized, double, yellow blend, high centered blooms are produced in great abundance by this little Floribunda. The production of both small and large clusters is nearly continuous on 'Daybreaker'.

FRAGRANCE: Very strong.

FORM & FOLIAGE: The foliage on this little sun lover starts out red and then turns dark, glossy green. It is very disease resistant.

WINTER PROTECTION: Full protection required. Easy rose to grow.

COMMENTS: "Tidy shrub with shiny, glossy leaves. Really floriferous, flowers last a long time. Love the foliage." "Nice rose."

Double Delight
Hybrid Tea

FLOWER: 'Double Delight' has large to very large, red blend, high centered, double blooms. The blooms start out creamy white splashed with strawberry red and gradually become redder. Each flower is unique. Flower production varies widely with some reporting continuous flowering and others having less success.

FRAGRANCE: Strong.

FORM & FOLIAGE: This is a bushy plant, 1 m (3 ft.) in height and width that likes lots of sun. The foliage is glossy but very prone to mildew.

WINTER PROTECTION: Full protection required. Difficult rose to grow.

COMMENTS: "Wonderful scent, intense and spicy." "Unusual colour and wonderful scent. Everyone who sees it wants one!" "Great for cutting. A beautiful rose, and is my favourite." 'Double Delight' has been both Queen of the Show and First Runner-Up at the Calgary Rose Show. However, results with 'Double Delight' are quite variable as some regard it as very easy to grow and suitable for novices while most find it challenging.

Dresden Doll

Miniature

FLOWER: 'Dresden Doll' produces small, cupped, semi-double flowers in a soft light pink. When fully open, the blooms display attractive golden stamens. The plant produces single blooms on mossy stems in several flushes throughout the summer.

FRAGRANCE: None to moderate.

FORM & FOLIAGE: In full sun this little rose forms a compact plant, 25 to 35 cm (10 to 15 in.) in height and width with glossy foliage and moss on all of the stems and buds. It has good disease resistance.

WINTER PROTECTION: Full protection required. Easy rose to grow.

COMMENTS: "Neat golden stamens. A pretty little bloomer. Love the Moss. Bloomed constantly." "I really like single roses, so this has become a favourite." 'Dresden Doll' is one of the better Moss Miniatures from Ralph Moore who struggled for almost 25 years to introduce the Moss Rose characteristics of the once-blooming Old Garden roses into repeat-flowering Miniature Roses.

Electron

Hybrid Tea

FLOWER: 'Electron' has large, deep pink, high centered, double blooms frequently produced in clusters of 3 or 4 blooms. Flower production is reduced in the shade.

FRAGRANCE: Moderate.

FORM & FOLIAGE: 'Electron', which has glossy, dark green foliage, is 1 m (3 ft.) in height and 60 cm (2 ft.) in width. It likes sun but can handle some shade. The stems are sturdy and the clusters of large blooms are held erect on the top of the plant. Foliage will burn if the plant is against a south-facing wall. Disease resistance is excellent.

WINTER PROTECTION: Full protection required. Average rose to grow.

COMMENTS: "Flowers open slowly and hold colour well, fading only slightly at the edges. Compact with very prickly stems. Electron is a reliable performer." "Beautiful form. Large flowers which last a long time." 'Electron' has been Queen of the Show or Best Pink Hybrid Tea several times at the Rose Show.

Empress Josephine (Impératrice Joséphine)

Gallica

FLOWER: The Old Garden rose 'Empress Josephine' produces medium pink, semi-double flowers that are medium sized and cupped in shape. The blooms are in small clusters. It flowers only once in mid summer. In wet weather the blooms will ball and not open properly.

FRAGRANCE: Moderate.

FORM & FOLIAGE: The plant will grow to about 1.2 m (4 ft.) in height and 1 m (3 ft.) in width. Black spot can bother the plant a little, but otherwise it is disease resistant. The stems are relatively free of thorns. The plant is well clothed in matte, greyish green leaves.

WINTER PROTECTION: Semi-hardy. Some winter protection required. Easy rose to grow.

COMMENTS: This rose was named after the Empress Josephine, wife of Napoleon, who collected all of the known roses of the world on her estate at Malmaison in France. This endeavour was so highly thought of that ships carrying nurserymen and specimens for her were allowed free passage even during the war between France and England.

Enfant de France
Hybrid Perpetual

FLOWER: The rose 'Enfant de France' has light pink, floppy, fragrant, very double blooms. It blooms in small clusters and repeats well.

FRAGRANCE: Very strong.

FORM & FOLIAGE: The bush will grow to about 1 m (3 ft.) in height and a little less in width. It likes lots of sun and is quite disease resistant. It has a vigorous growth habit.

WINTER PROTECTION: Semi-hardy. Some winter protection required. Easy rose to grow.

COMMENTS: "Sweet fragrance. Silvery pink cast to the flowers. Pretty tough. Survived an ugly move." "Came back after being driven over three times by teenagers in the middle of winter. What a little toughie. I love this rose." 'Enfant de France' was introduced just before the development of the Hybrid Teas so it has always had to compete with them. The fact that it has competed and survived shows what a delight it is.

English Miss
Floribunda

FLOWER: This little rose produces flushes of large, light pink, double blooms in small clusters throughout the summer. Although the blooms start out high centered, they open wide to reveal golden yellow stamens.

FRAGRANCE: Moderate.

FORM & FOLIAGE: 'English Miss' is a dainty little bush, barely 45 cm (1.5 ft.) in height and 30 cm (1 ft.) in width. With its glossy foliage, it likes to be in full sun. Unfortunately, black spot can occur on this rose.

WINTER PROTECTION: Full protection required. Average rose to grow.

COMMENTS: "We planted this rose in 2003 and it seems to have lost some of its vigour over time."

Europeana
Floribunda

FLOWER: 'Europeana' produces armfuls of dark, crimson red flowers in large clusters. The blooms are numerous, small to medium sized and rosette shaped, but the individual blooms are lost in the overall mass effect. The added weight of any rain may weigh down some of the sprays.

FRAGRANCE: Mild to moderate.

FORM & FOLIAGE: The plants are well branched and vigorous with lots of glossy foliage. Because of the weight of the large sprays of flowers, the stems often droop and the plant therefore grows as wide as it is tall, about 75 to 90 cm (2.5 to 3 ft.). Flowering is most abundant when the plant has full sun. 'Europeana' may be very prone to powdery mildew.

WINTER PROTECTION: Full protection required. Average rose to grow.

COMMENTS: "'Europeana' is an older variety, but still the best red Floribunda on the market." "Lots of large bright clusters, reliable performer, strong grower. Flowers retain their colour and last a long time." It has been the winner of 8 trophies at the Calgary Rose Show.

Evelyn

English

FLOWER: 'Evelyn' blooms in flushes that run together to be almost continuous through the summer. The blooms are apricot blend, but become pinker later in the summer. The shape of the blooms is cupped and double and they are produced in small clusters.

FRAGRANCE: Strong.

FORM & FOLIAGE: The tall upright bushes with glossy, medium green foliage will grow to 1 m (3 ft.) in height and 60 cm (2 ft.) in width. 'Evelyn' likes lots of sun, but avoid really hot areas of the garden as the heat will cause the blooms to fade. Black spot can sometimes be a problem. Water well and evenly for stronger necks.

WINTER PROTECTION: Full protection required. Average rose to grow.

COMMENTS: "Beautiful Old Garden rose type blooms of good substance, which last a long time on the plant or in the vase. Fabulous fragrance. Strong upright bush." Named on behalf of Crabtree & Evelyn, who used it in their range of rose perfumes. Creator David Austin says that "Evelyn's great glory is its wonderful fragrance, which is similar in style to an Old Rose but with a sumptuous fruity note reminiscent of fresh peaches and apricot."

Fantin-Latour

Centifolia

FLOWER: The light pink flowers on 'Fantin-Latour' are quartered rosettes with about a hundred petals. The blooms at first are cupped, but then the outer petals relax to expose a central button of tightly packed smaller petals. It blooms on old wood.

FRAGRANCE: Strong.

FORM & FOLIAGE: The plant will grow to about 1.2 m (4 ft.) in height and width. It tends to be a floppy plant so it needs a lot of room.

WINTER PROTECTION: Semi-hardy. Some winter protection required. Canes should be covered. Average rose to grow.

COMMENTS: "Sweet fragrance." "Blooms last a long time. Plant flowers until August. Superb fragrance." "If pruning is needed, prune after flowering is finished for the summer." Ignace Fantin-Latour (1836 – 1904) was a famous French artist renowned for his paintings of flowers.

First Prize

Hybrid Tea

FLOWER: 'First Prize' has gorgeous, very large, silvery pink blend, high centered blooms on long stems with occasional small clusters. The number of blooms is quite variable from one plant to the next.

FRAGRANCE: Strong.

FORM & FOLIAGE: The plant is tall and upright, growing up to 1.2 m (4 ft.) in height and 75 cm (2.5 ft.) in width with glossy dark green foliage. It likes the sun.

WINTER PROTECTION: Full protection required. Easy rose to grow.

COMMENTS: "Very strong, great exhibition rose. Colour bleaches out as the bloom ages." "Very vigorous growth, huge flowers." "Quality makes up for the small quantity of blooms. Huge, absolutely stunning flowers."

Folklore
Hybrid Tea

FLOWER: 'Folklore' produces large, classic high centre, orange and orange blend blossoms in singles and small clusters.

FRAGRANCE: Mild to moderate.

FORM & FOLIAGE: This rose grows tall and slim and is 1.2 to 1.8 m (4 to 6 ft.) in height. Its foliage is abundant and glossy, but sometimes prone to mildew. The plant prefers full sun.

WINTER PROTECTION: Full protection required. Difficult rose to grow.

COMMENTS: "Vigorous grower, tall, beautiful, long lasting blooms which are great for cutting. 'Folklore' is a consistent performer." 'Folklore' won Queen of the Show in 2003 at the Calgary Rose Show and has also won for Best Hybrid Tea spray. The blooms are frequent entrants in the Rose in a Bowl and English Box classes.

Fragrant Cloud
Hybrid Tea

FLOWER: 'Fragrant Cloud' produces large, double blooms of orange-red or coral-red that start out high centered then become cupped. Many flowers have muddled centers. It is very floriferous, mostly with small sprays, but some single blossoms may be available for cutting.

FRAGRANCE: Very strong.

FORM & FOLIAGE: 'Fragrant Cloud' grows up to 1 m (3 ft.) in height and 75 cm (2.5 ft.) in width. Its leaves are large and glossy with average disease resistance. The plants can handle some shade, but also do very well against the south side of a house.

WINTER PROTECTION: Full protection required. Easy rose to grow.

COMMENTS: "Blooms last well on the plant, but the colour does fade a little after a few days." "Very strong fragrance." "Enough single blooms to cut and give away and leave the clusters for show in the garden. Quick repeat." "These are not classic shapes for the annual show, but the fragrance is so wonderful that I love it." 'Fragrant Cloud' is a frequent winner of the Most Fragrant Rose trophy at the Calgary Rose Show.

Garden Party
Hybrid Tea

FLOWER: 'Garden Party' has large, double, high centered blooms that are white with a touch of pink. The plant repeats well with moderate bloom production in small clusters with a few single blooms. The blooms on 'Garden Party' have better tolerance to rain than most white roses.

FRAGRANCE: Moderate.

FORM & FOLIAGE: This is a vigorous, mid-sized bush up to 1 m (3 ft.) in height and 60 cm (2 ft.) in width which likes lots of sun, in a warm but not a hot place. Its foliage is glossy but is particularly prone to mildew.

WINTER PROTECTION: Full protection required. Easy rose to grow.

COMMENTS: "Love the blooms." "Beautiful flowers with wavy petals in ivory white." "Give it proper care as 'Garden Party' is prone to mildew if not given enough space." "Blooms last a long time on the bush."

George Burns · *Floribunda*

FLOWER: The medium sized blooms on 'George Burns' are officially classed as yellow blend. On the plant they start out as pale yellow with pink to red stripes and flecks and gradually fade to white with pink stripes and flecks. The clusters of semi-double blooms provide a bright splash in two very long lasting flushes per year.

FRAGRANCE: Moderate.

FORM & FOLIAGE: 'George Burns' is a sturdy plant that grows to about 1 m (3 ft.) in height and 75 cm (2.5 ft.) in width. This is a rose that can get by with less sun than most roses. It can occasionally get a little mildew or black spot.

WINTER PROTECTION: Full protection required. Average rose to grow.

COMMENTS: "Love the colour and fragrance of this rose. Two major flushes of blooms per year. Has rather nasty thorns." "Sometimes it had so many flowers I had to stake up the branches." "Love it. Very showy." "Most years it grows high and bushy, but did not like our hot summer last year and did not grow well."

Gizmo · *Miniature*

FLOWER: The plant is covered with cupped to flat 5 cm (2 in.) diameter single blooms in an orange red colour with a white eye. 'Gizmo' is the closest you can get to a continuous bloomer among the miniature roses. The blooms will spot in the rain. 'Gizmo' is best grown for mass effect, rather than the beauty of individual blooms. Blooms stay on the plant for a long time and gradually fade to pale orange.

FRAGRANCE: None.

FORM & FOLIAGE: This rose has glossy foliage that is immune to everything except the occasional trace of black spot. It prefers lots of sun, but will still bloom in some shade. It grows to about 30 cm (1 ft.) tall and 45 cm (1.5 ft.) wide.

WINTER PROTECTION: Minor winter protection required. Easy rose to grow.

COMMENTS: "Fast repeater. Cutie, unusual shade of orange." "Bloomed continuously from late June to mid October, at times with 50 to 70 blooms on it."

Gold Medal · *Grandiflora*

FLOWER: The blooms on 'Gold Medal' will vary in colour from medium yellow to rich golden yellow and occasionally have a tinge of pink. The colour variation occurs from plant to plant, and sometimes from flush to flush on the same plant. All of the blooms are classic high centre doubles, in singles and small clusters, on long stems. Flushes last a long time, but the plants are less floriferous than some other roses.

FRAGRANCE: Faint.

FORM & FOLIAGE: The plants are quite large, up to 1 to 1.2 m (3 to 4 ft.) in height and 60 cm (2 ft.) in width. It has good disease resistance, but it can sometimes get a little black spot or mildew. It likes full sun.

WINTER PROTECTION: Full protection required. Average rose to grow.

COMMENTS: "Sweet and pleasant fragrance." "Colour fades to white. Often the last of the tender roses to be blooming in the garden in the fall." "Individual blooms can be absolutely stunning when they first open." "Love this rose. When it first blooms, the gold colour is beautiful."

Gourmet Popcorn
Miniature

FLOWER: 'Gourmet Popcorn' has large sprays of small, pure white blooms with golden yellow stamens. This little plant flowers continuously and produces a large number of semi-double blooms in a season.

FRAGRANCE: Slight.

FORM & FOLIAGE: This rose is a sun lover with glossy, medium green foliage. It does sometimes get a little mildew. It will grow to 45 cm (1.5 ft.) in height and 30 cm (1 ft.) in width.

WINTER PROTECTION: Full protection required. Easy rose to grow.

COMMENTS: "Great bloomer. Lovely rose." "Blooms last a long time. This is one of my larger bush size minis. It is also one of my favourites."

Heritage
English

FLOWER: Usually 'Heritage' produces small clusters of medium sized, light pink blooms, but occasionally it will produce a very large cluster. The blooms are cupped, double and produced in great profusion throughout the summer.

FRAGRANCE: Strong.

FORM & FOLIAGE: The plant likes lots of sun for its glossy, dark green foliage. Black spot rarely affects this rose. 'Heritage' requires a little more pruning than normal because it is such a prolific grower. It grows to 1 m (3 ft.) tall and nearly as wide.

WINTER PROTECTION: Full protection required. Easy rose to grow.

COMMENTS: "Gorgeous, light pink OGR type blooms. Scent has hint of lemon. Great in vase. Heads do not flop if well watered." "Few thorns. Vigorous shrub. Branches bend with the weight of the flowers. This rose is really hardy. I planted this rose when I knew nothing about roses and never winterized it. Tall and lanky." "Holds form and colour in weather." "This rose is reported to be David Austin's personal favourite."

Honey Perfume
Floribunda

FLOWER: 'Honey Perfume' produces medium sized, apricot blend flowers in small clusters throughout the summer. The blooms are semi-double.

FRAGRANCE: Mild.

FORM & FOLIAGE: This small Floribunda, growing only to about 45 cm (1.5 ft.) in height and width, likes all the sun it can get. The glossy foliage is very disease resistant.

WINTER PROTECTION: Full protection required. Average rose to grow.

COMMENTS: "The flowers last a long time in the garden." "This is my favourite tender rose. I really love this rose's disease resistance and beauty." "Neat colour. Nice fragrance." 'Honey Perfume' was released in 2004 and has been evaluated in only a few Calgary gardens. While it drew rave reviews in some gardens, it did not grow well in others.

Hot Tamale

Miniature

FLOWER: 'Hot Tamale' produces abundant high centered, double blooms in flushes throughout the summer and is seldom out of bloom. The flowers are bright yellow and red, gradually fading to pink and white. The plant produces both single blooms and large clusters. The blooms are classic high center, double and stand upright on stems that are suitable for cutting.

FRAGRANCE: Faint.

FORM & FOLIAGE: The bush will grow to about 45 cm (1.5 ft.) in height and 30 cm (1 ft.) in width with a rather sprawling shape. There is not a lot of glossy foliage as the plant concentrates on bloom production. 'Hot Tamale' can occasionally get mildew or black spot.

WINTER PROTECTION: Full protection required. Easy rose to grow.

COMMENTS: "Bright, cheerful, undemanding little plant. Puts on a nice garden show. Occasionally get single blooms that are nice to cut." 'Hot Tamale' is one of the most popular miniature roses in Canada.

Iceberg

Floribunda

FLOWER: 'Iceberg' produces masses of pure white flowers which start out high centered and quickly open wide to reveal the golden stamens. Bloom production is excellent in flushes all summer. The blooms are semi-double to double and occur in both small and large clusters. Rain will sometimes cause spots on the petals of the blooms, a common problem with white roses.

FRAGRANCE: Moderate.

FORM & FOLIAGE: 'Iceberg' does not grow as large in Calgary as pictures in many books show for other areas. Typical size for the plants in Calgary is 60 to 75 cm (2 to 2.5 ft.) in height and width. It likes lots of sun and is usually free of disease.

WINTER PROTECTION: Full protection required. Average rose to grow.

COMMENTS: "Pure white blooms." "It is a beautiful classic rose bush. Best white Floribunda ever." "Flowers are smaller than most, but there are lots of them. A nice showy plant." "Colour holds—for a white rose. This rose has been rated as one of the most free flowering of roses!" "In some gardens, 'Iceberg' gets black spot."

Jacqueline du Pré

Shrub

FLOWER: The large, wide, semi-double, cupped white blooms of 'Jacqueline du Pré' sometimes have a pinkish reverse. Flower production is good in flushes and the blooms occur in small clusters. The stamens are made up of bright red filaments and golden yellow anthers, creating an unusual and very colourful effect in each flower. The blooms open to a cupped shape and then open further to be almost flat.

FRAGRANCE: Moderate.

FORM & FOLIAGE: This plant can grow over 1 m (3 ft.) in height, but only about 60 cm (2 ft.) in width. Its foliage is glossy and it has average disease resistance. It will grow in some shade, but will produce fewer flowers.

WINTER PROTECTION: Full protection required. Average rose to grow.

COMMENTS: "I love this rose!! It makes a statement like few roses can. Starts flowering early and repeats well." "Petals glow—mine was almost a light mauve." "Lemon musk fragrance. Neat yellow stamens." "Tall girl. 'Jacqueline du Pré' taught me that semi-double roses are beautiful."

Jeanne Lajoie

Miniature Climber

FLOWER: 'Jeanne Lajoie' produces large numbers of small, medium pink blooms in flushes throughout the summer. It needs to be deadheaded after the first flush to encourage more bloom production in the later flushes. The double blooms are high centered to begin and open to a cupped shape. The flowers occur as singles and as small and large clusters over the entire plant.

FRAGRANCE: None to faint.

FORM & FOLIAGE: 'Jeanne Lajoie' is an adaptable plant. It can be pruned to be tall and narrow, or to be short and wide. If protected through the winter, the plants can grow to 1.2 m (4 ft.) in height. The glossy foliage is quite resistant to mildew, but can develop black spot.

WINTER PROTECTION: Full protection required. Easy rose to grow.

COMMENTS: "Very pretty." "Sends up new growth each year." "Because of die back, never reaches its potential in size in the short season in Calgary." "Beautiful little climber." "Can tolerate some shade, but produces less blooms." One four-year-old plant produced over 200 blooms in a summer.

Joyfulness

Hybrid Tea

FLOWER: The large, high centered blooms are apricot blend with a pink blush on the edges of the petals. The flower production of 'Joyfulness' is good in flushes with both singles and small clusters of blooms.

FRAGRANCE: Faint.

FORM & FOLIAGE: 'Joyfulness' can grow over 1 m (3 ft.) in height and 75 cm (2.5 ft.) in width in the right setting with lots of sun. Its foliage is glossy. Although 'Joyfulness' demonstrates good disease resistance, it is still susceptible to mildew.

WINTER PROTECTION: Full protection. Easy to average rose to grow.

COMMENTS: "Wonderful exhibition form, but colour fades. Very beautiful rose, really enjoy having it in my garden. Its name reflects its beauty. One of my favourites." "A very pretty rose."

Königin von Dänemark (Queen of Denmark)

Alba

FLOWER: This famous old rose, introduced in 1826, produces medium pink, flat, sometimes quartered blooms in such profusion they weigh down the branches. The colour is dark pink as the flowers open from fat, flat topped buds and then fades as the bloom matures, although the center of the bloom stays darker than the edges. 'Königin von Dänemark' blooms once only, but has quite a long bloom period. Sporadic rebloom has been noted.

FRAGRANCE: Strong.

FORM & FOLIAGE: This rose does not get very large in Calgary due to the short growing season. It grows only to about 60 – 75 cm (2 – 2.5 ft.) in height and 45 cm (1.5 ft.) in width. Its disease resistance is good. On its own roots it will sucker to form a dense patch.

WINTER PROTECTION: Semi-hardy. Some winter protection required. Average rose to grow.

COMMENTS: "One of the few pink Albas." "Sweet, exquisite fragrance."

L.D. Braithwaite

English

FLOWER: The large, dark red flowers on 'L.D. Braithwaite' are held erect on strong stems, so that when in full bloom, the shrub produces an eye catching display. The blooms are open-cupped, each on its own stem and do not fade. Flower production is very good throughout the summer in a nearly continuous display. Heavy continuous rain can cause balling.

FRAGRANCE: Faint to moderate.

FORM & FOLIAGE: While the plant likes full sun, it can get by in partial shade, but with decreased bloom production. The foliage is glossy and usually trouble free. Plants will grow 1–1.2 m (3–4 ft.) in height and a little less in width.

WINTER PROTECTION: Full protection required. Easy to average rose to grow.

COMMENTS: "The best English rose I have grown. Strong neck, weatherproof, very vigorous and hardy."

La Ville de Bruxelles

Damask

FLOWER: Large, deep pink, very double blooms are produced in abundance in mid-summer. 'La Ville de Bruxelles' has no repeat bloom. The flat flowers fade a little around the edges when fully open.

FRAGRANCE: Strong.

FORM & FOLIAGE: The growth is strong, vigorous and upright to about 1 m (3 ft.). This rose is quite disease resistant.

WINTER PROTECTION: Semi-hardy. Some winter protection required. Average rose to grow.

COMMENTS: "Beautiful quartered pink blooms. Flat, huge bright flowers. Strong—the Incredible Hulk. What a star!" "One of the best of the Old Garden roses." "Sweet fragrance."

Liebeszauber (Crimson Spire)

Hybrid Tea

FLOWER: Medium red blooms of good size occur in singles and small clusters. Some blooms are high centered, but blooms with muddled centers are common. Flower production is good with long lasting flushes.

FRAGRANCE: Moderate.

FORM & FOLIAGE: 'Liebeszauber' is a tall, narrow plant which grows to 1.2 m (4 ft.) tall and 60 cm (2 ft.) wide with glossy foliage that is reddish when young, dark green when mature. It likes the sun and does well on the south side of a house. 'Liebeszauber' can get some black spot, but is not bothered by it and continues to grow and produce flowers.

WINTER PROTECTION: Full protection required. Average rose to grow.

COMMENTS: "Pleasant fragrance." "Exceptional strong, thick canes with large, dark, healthy leaves. Consistent performer." "Vigorous."

Louise Odier

Bourbon

FLOWER: The deep pink, very double blooms of 'Louise Odier' are cupped at first, and then become flat and round. This is one of the most floriferous of the Old Garden roses. The repeat bloom is very good. The medium sized flowers are produced in loose bunches on long stems.

FRAGRANCE: Strong.

FORM & FOLIAGE: 'Louise Odier' has a lot of pale to mid-green leaves on a sometimes lax but vigorous plant. The stems are thick and prickly and the plant will grow to 1.5 m (5 ft.) in height and 1 m (3 ft.) in width. Its disease resistance is good and it tolerates some shade.

WINTER PROTECTION: Semi-hardy. Some winter protection required. Average rose to grow.

COMMENTS: "Deliciously fragrant." "Hubba, Hubba, what a rose. Neat flowers. Good re-bloomer. Will do shade. Good in a vase."

Love and Peace

Hybrid Tea

FLOWER: The large blooms of 'Love and Peace' are classified as yellow blend but are bright yellow in the center and deep pink around the outside edge. It is a real eye catcher in the garden. The blooms are double and start out high centered, but as the flowers open they very often reveal a muddled center. The blossoms are nearly always singles on long stems.

FRAGRANCE: Faint to strong.

FORM & FOLIAGE: 'Love and Peace' produces a vigorous, strong plant which grows very upright to 1 m (3 ft.) in height and 60 cm (2 ft.) in width. The rose is well covered with large, very glossy leaves that are sometimes susceptible to mildew and black spot. It likes full sun.

WINTER PROTECTION: Full protection required. Average rose to grow.

COMMENTS: "Although this rose has a lot of blooms, they usually have a confused center and are not exhibition quality." "Spectacular blooms but only 4 to 6 at a time."

Love

Grandiflora

FLOWER: The large, high centered blooms are red with a silver reverse and are classified as red blends. Each bloom is on its own stem. The flowers appear in flushes throughout the summer, but flowering is not as abundant as some other roses.

FRAGRANCE: None to strong.

FORM & FOLIAGE: This sun loving rose with glossy foliage will grow to 1 m (3 ft.) in height and 60 cm (2 ft.) in width. 'Love' may be susceptible to aphids, mildew and black spot in some gardens.

WINTER PROTECTION: Full protection required. Difficult rose to grow.

COMMENTS: "Very tight buds, white reverse." "Very showy." "This rose was planted in 1999. It seemed to struggle at first but in the last few years has become stronger and has produced more flowers. 2006 was the best year yet." "This rose lost vigor with age until it was the size of a mini so it was shovel pruned."

Madame Hardy   *Damask*

FLOWER: 'Madame Hardy' is very generous with its one flush of very double, pure white flowers in early summer. Pink tinged buds open to cup shaped blooms that flatten out. The blooms occur in singles and small clusters. It blooms on the previous year's growth.

FRAGRANCE: Strong.

FORM & FOLIAGE: This is a tall, dense, prickly shrub that grows to about 1.2 m (4 ft.) in height. It can tolerate some shade, but will bloom better in full sun. It is generally very healthy, with matte, medium green leaves.

WINTER PROTECTION: Semi-hardy. Some winter protection required. Canes should be covered. Easy rose to grow.

COMMENTS: "Big flowers. Pretty shrub." "Blooms are long lasting and pure white with a green eye. Add magnesium sulphate to prevent chlorosis." "Exceptional fragrance." This is one of the most beautiful of all roses according to Peter Beales in *A Passion for Roses*.

Maiden's Blush (Great Maiden's Blush, Cuisse de Nymphe)   *Alba*

FLOWER: Blooms are white or delicate flesh pink and are loosely double and globular. The blooms are followed by long orange hips. It does not repeat.

FRAGRANCE: Moderate.

FORM & FOLIAGE: 'Maiden's Blush' is graceful and arching to about 1 m (3 ft.) in height and 60 cm (2 ft.) in width. Its foliage is bluish grey green and often puckered or crinkled. It can sometimes suffer from black spot. The plant can handle some shade.

WINTER PROTECTION: Semi-hardy. Some winter protection required. Easy rose to grow.

COMMENTS: "Variable fragrance has been described as sweet, refined, evocative and divine." "It is tough, hardy, and adaptable." Peter Beales comments that if he were allowed to take just one rose with him to solitary confinement on some far-off desert island, Maiden's Blush would most certainly be his choice. The French name for the rose translates as Nymph's Thigh.

Margaret Merril   *Floribunda*

FLOWER: White, medium to large, semi-double to double blooms are borne in continuous flushes, so 'Margaret Merril' seems to be nearly always in bloom. The blooms are high centered at first, but open wide. Blooming is prolific in small clusters. Rain causes only a little spotting on the petals.

FRAGRANCE: Moderate to strong.

FORM & FOLIAGE: 'Margaret Merril' likes lots of sun, but can tolerate shade for part of the day. The foliage is glossy and can sometimes get a little black spot. It will grow to about 1 m (3 ft.) in height and 75 cm (2.5 ft.) in width.

WINTER PROTECTION: Full protection required. Average rose to grow.

COMMENTS: "Wonderful fragrance, very pleasing. Grew and bloomed well on the east side of house. Put it beside our front door so we can enjoy the fragrance and the number of blooms." "The flowers are very beautiful when fully blown and they last a long time on the bush." "Keeps on flowering. A solid rose."

Marijke Koopman
Hybrid Tea

FLOWER: 'Marijke Koopman' produces medium pink blooms with a classic high centre. The blooms are mostly singles with a few small clusters borne in flushes throughout the summer.

FRAGRANCE: None to moderate.

FORM & FOLIAGE: The bush grows to about 1.2 m (4 ft.) in height with very thin stems which still manage to hold the flowers erect. This rose may be susceptible to mildew, but has good resistance to black spot.

WINTER PROTECTION: Full protection required. Average rose to grow.

COMMENTS: "Reliable performer, long pointed buds, elegant rose, long lasting flowers."

Marilyn Monroe
Hybrid Tea

FLOWER: 'Marilyn Monroe' has large, high centered, double, apricot blend blooms that appear continuously. Its flower production is excellent.

FRAGRANCE: Moderate.

FORM & FOLIAGE: This rose likes the sun but will still bloom with only 4 hours of morning sun. It grows to about 1 m (3 ft.) in height, but only 45 cm (1 ft.) in width. It has average disease resistance.

WINTER PROTECTION: Full protection required. Easy rose to grow.

COMMENTS: "Great bloomer. Holds its shape for a long time. Won me so many awards and trophies it is unbelievable."

Mary Rose
English

FLOWER: This rose produces medium sized, medium pink, very double, cupped flowers in small clusters. The plants produce two major flushes of blooms per summer, but are seldom without blooms.

FRAGRANCE: Faint to moderate.

FORM & FOLIAGE: The foliage is dark green with a matte surface and has excellent disease resistance. It will grow to about 1 m (3 ft.) in height and 75 cm (2.5 ft.) in width. The canes are very thorny.

WINTER PROTECTION: Full protection required. Easy rose to grow.

COMMENTS: "I love the pink blooms of this rose." 'Mary Rose' is among the easiest of the English roses to grow and is one of the most widely grown.

Minnie Pearl

Miniature

FLOWER: 'Minnie Pearl' has delicate, pale, pink blend, double flowers with classic high centers. Each bloom is light pink with a darker pink reverse. The blooms are mostly singles with a few small clusters in flushes throughout the summer. 'Minnie Pearl' does not give the mass show of colour that some other mini roses provide. Rain can cause minor spotting to the blooms.

FRAGRANCE: None.

FORM & FOLIAGE: This is a fairly wide spreading plant that likes all the sun it can get. It is usually disease resistant but the semi-glossy foliage can sometimes get a little black spot. It will grow to about 40 cm (1.3 ft.) in height and width.

WINTER PROTECTION: Full protection required. Easy rose to grow.

COMMENTS: "Very pretty rose." "Love the beautiful little pink blooms." 'Minnie Pearl' has for over twenty years been one of the highest rated miniature roses.

Miss All-American Beauty (Maria Callas)

Hybrid Tea

FLOWER: 'Miss All-American Beauty' produces very large, high centered to cupped blooms in deep pink. The plants produce well in flushes of single blooms and small clusters.

FRAGRANCE: Very strong.

FORM & FOLIAGE: This vigorous, upright, bushy plant with dark green foliage will grow to 1.2 m (4 ft.) in height. It has average disease resistance and prefers lots of sun.

WINTER PROTECTION: Full protection required. Average plant to grow.

COMMENTS: "Consistent colour, reliable performer." "'Miss All-American Beauty' has very large, exhibition shaped blooms. The colour is a wonderful pink."

Olympiad

Hybrid Tea

FLOWER: 'Olympiad' has beautiful, large, medium red, double flowers. Intervals between flushes are quite short so throughout the summer the plants are usually in bloom. Often the first flowers of the season are singles on long stems, while the later flushes produce more clusters.

FRAGRANCE: None to faint.

FORM & FOLIAGE: 'Olympiad' is a strong plant with exuberant growth and will grow 1 to 1.2 m (3 to 4 ft.) in height with glossy foliage. While it likes lots of sun, it can handle some shade. It has very good disease resistance.

WINTER PROTECTION: Full protection required. Easy rose to grow.

COMMENTS: "Fruity fragrance, if any. Long lasting flowers on the bush or cut. Strong, long stems." "Reliable performer. Excellent cut rose. Healthy plant." "Likes a cooler place in your garden for nicer colour." "It has been the first rose in my garden to flower in spring." "Olympiad was the official rose of the 1984 Los Angeles Olympics." 'Olympiad' is a great winner at the annual show having won Queen, Princess, and Best Hybrid Tea spray trophies.

Pandemonium
Miniature

FLOWER: The flowers of 'Pandemonium' are a wild mixture of stripes and flecks of vibrant orange and yellow with no two blooms the same. The floppy, semi-double blooms are classed as a yellow blend. Flowering is mostly as single blooms with the occasional small cluster, scattered all over the plant. It blooms in long lasting flushes, with only short breaks between the flushes.

FRAGRANCE: Faint.

FORM & FOLIAGE: This is a strong growing plant that some books classify as a patio rose, or even as a Floribunda. In Calgary, it grows as a large mini reaching a height and width of up to 45 cm (1.5 ft.). The foliage is glossy, medium green and has good resistance to disease.

WINTER PROTECTION: Full protection required. Average rose to grow.

COMMENTS: "We had a hanging basket of 'Pandemoniums'. They grew rather upright, and bloomed and bloomed all summer." "If you want something to catch people's attention, this rose is for you."

Pascali
Hybrid Tea

FLOWER: 'Pascali' has pure white blooms of medium to large size that open from very small buds. The classic, high centered blooms are usually in small clusters so the plants need to have the side buds removed if you want large single stem flowers for the house or the show. Blooms stand up well to rain, but can occasionally spot.

FRAGRANCE: Faint to moderate.

FORM & FOLIAGE: 'Pascali' is a tall, narrow, upright plant that will grow to over 1 m (3 ft.) in height. Aphids seem to like 'Pascali' and the plant can sometimes suffer from black spot.

WINTER PROTECTION: Full protection required. Easy rose to grow.

COMMENTS: "Colour does not fade." 'Pascali' has been around since 1963 and is still one of the best white Hybrid Tea roses available. 'Pascali' may be less vigorous in Calgary than other Hybrid Tea roses.

Peace
Hybrid Tea

FLOWER: 'Peace' has very large, high center, double blooms produced in flushes throughout the summer. The golden yellow petals have pale pink edges. Flower production is quite variable, depending on the care given and the age of the plant. The first flush is usually all single blooms on long stems, but later flushes contain more small clusters of blooms.

FRAGRANCE: Moderate.

FORM & FOLIAGE: Plants tend to grow to only about 75 cm (2.5 ft.) in height and 60 cm (2 ft.) in width in Calgary, smaller than in most other places. 'Peace' has large glossy leaves and likes lots of sun. It sometimes suffers from black spot.

WINTER PROTECTION: Full protection required. Easy rose to grow.

COMMENTS: "Really pleased with its classic, round, high center bloom and its yellow with pink edges. I like the way each petal edge folds back. Nice foliage." "An oldie but a must if you want to grow Hybrid Tea roses." "Did well for first couple of years and then gradually faded away."

Peacekeeper

Floribunda

FLOWER: Although the blooms of 'Peacekeeper' are officially classified as pink blend, they are orange with shades to yellow. The small, double, high centered blooms open wide as they age. Flower production is prolific and blooms are produced in large clusters in flushes through the summer.

FRAGRANCE: Moderate.

FORM & FOLIAGE: 'Peacekeeper' grows to about 75 cm (2.5 ft.) in height and 60 cm (2 ft.) in width with light green glossy foliage. This rose likes all the sun it can get and has good disease resistance.

WINTER PROTECTION: Full protection required. Average rose to grow.

COMMENTS: "'Peacekeeper' is a keeper, a lovely little miniature 'Peace' rose." "This is a rose to add a spot of bright colour to a garden." "I love this rose and my garden will never be without it."

Pink Parfait

Floribunda/Grandiflora

FLOWER: 'Pink Parfait' has medium sized, pink blend flowers that start out with high centers and then open wide. It produces several flushes of two-tone double blooms in small clusters throughout the summer.

FRAGRANCE: Very faint.

FORM & FOLIAGE: The foliage is medium green and crinkled. 'Pink Parfait' is very disease resistant. It will grow to about 75 cm (2.5 ft.) in height and 60 cm (2 ft.) in width.

WINTER PROTECTION: Full protection required. Easy rose to grow.

COMMENTS: "Very nice rose. Holds colour and form. First blooms have a form close to a Hybrid Tea. Give it lots of sun and water." In September, 1998, the Montreal Botanical Garden carried out a survey of its roses' resistance to black spot, powdery mildew and rust. 'Pink Parfait' was one of the best with an infection rate of only 0% to 5%.

Playboy (Cheerio)

Floribunda

FLOWER: 'Playboy' has yellow gold blooms tinged with red that fade to pink. The flowers are medium to large, floppy, singles produced in small and large clusters. The plant blooms in flushes with a very fast repeat. Heavy rain will knock off the petals, but the plant produces more flowers quickly. The American Rose Society lists 'Playboy' as a red blend, while the Canadian Rose Society lists it as orange blend.

FRAGRANCE: Very faint.

FORM & FOLIAGE: 'Playboy' is very disease resistant. The glossy foliage with the bright blooms makes for a very attractive plant. If it is given full sun and lots of water, it should grow to about 1 m (3 ft.) in height and 75 cm (2.5 ft.) in width.

WINTER PROTECTION: Full protection required. Average rose to grow.

COMMENTS: "Yes, he really is a 'Playboy'. Once cut, he keeps dropping his petals at every opportunity so not a good show rose. Gorgeous colour. Holds colour well. Very quick to reflower." "I was not a fan of single blooms until I got 'Playboy'. It is one of the showiest plants in the garden."

Pristine
Hybrid Tea

FLOWER: The large, white blooms of 'Pristine' have touches of pink. The classic, high center blooms grow as singles and small clusters in flushes throughout the summer. Pristine is not as floriferous as some other Hybrid Teas.

FRAGRANCE: None to moderate.

FORM & FOLIAGE: In Calgary, the bushes grow to only about 60 cm (2 ft.) in height and 45 cm (1.5 ft.) in width, much smaller than in many other places. The plants, which like full sun, have large canes and glossy foliage, but can get a little black spot in some summers.

WINTER PROTECTION: Full protection required. Easy rose to grow.

COMMENTS: "Its name says it all!" "Does not produce many blooms." 'Pristine' has won Queen of the Show and Best White Hybrid Tea each three times at the Calgary Rose Show. It is sometimes a little difficult to find a supplier for 'Pristine'.

Queen Elizabeth
Grandiflora

FLOWER: 'Queen Elizabeth' produces medium to large, high centered, pale pink blooms on a tall, narrow plant. The blooms are usually in small clusters, but both long stemmed single flowers and larger clusters do occur. Flower production is usually good.

FRAGRANCE: Faint.

FORM & FOLIAGE: This is a tall, narrow plant that grows over 1 m (3 ft.) in height and 45 cm (1.5 ft.) in width. This sun-loving rose is usually quite disease resistant, but the aphids sometimes find the glossy foliage to their liking.

WINTER PROTECTION: Full protection required. Easy to average rose to grow.

COMMENTS: "'Queen Elizabeth' is one of the best roses in my garden." "Flower production was not so good." The Grandiflora class was created for the Queen Elizabeth rose. It was the first rose that had the plant size and high centred blooms of a Hybrid Tea, but which bloomed in clusters like a Floribunda.

Rainbow's End
Miniature

FLOWER: The flowers on 'Rainbow's End' are classed as yellow blend and if the blooms are produced in the shade, or in the house, they will be a pure golden yellow, perhaps with a trace of red. In full sun, the 5 cm (2 in.) blooms start mostly yellow then quickly become red or red and yellow, fading to white. A prolific bloomer, it is common to find all three colours on the plant at the same time, sometimes within the same cluster. The many petalled flowers are high centered and fully double.

FRAGRANCE: None.

FORM & FOLIAGE: An upright and sturdy plant, it will grow to about 40 cm (1.3 ft.) in height and width. It can be bothered by black spot in some gardens.

WINTER PROTECTION: Full protection required. Easy rose to grow.

COMMENTS: "A very rewarding rose to grow. Plants can be started from cuttings." "A lovely little rose with many fans."

Rosa Mundi (R. gallica versicolor) — *Gallica*

FLOWER: While classified as a pink blend, the blooms on 'Rosa Mundi' are actually pink or red and white striped. The small clusters of large, semi-double flowers come in one flush in mid-summer. There is no repeat. Blooms are produced on old wood.

FRAGRANCE: Moderate to strong.

FORM & FOLIAGE: 'Rosa Mundi' will grow to about 1 m (3 ft.) in height and 75 cm (2.5 ft.) in width. If grown in shade, there is a reduction in bloom production. The plant is healthy while in flower, but gets some mildew later and aphids seem to like it.

WINTER PROTECTION: Semi-hardy. Some winter protection required. Canes should be covered. Average rose to grow.

COMMENTS: "Dip a blush pink rose in berry juice, then shake it and this is what you get. Very interesting colour combination." By far the most popular of the Gallica Roses, 'Rosa Mundi' is about 300 years old.

Rosemary Harkness — *Hybrid Tea*

FLOWER: 'Rosemary Harkness' has medium sized, semi-double, orange pink blooms that start high centered and open wide to reveal the stamens. Single blooms and small clusters are spread all over the plant in a nearly continuous display.

FRAGRANCE: Faint to moderate.

FORM & FOLIAGE: 'Rosemary Harkness' is bushy and grows to 1 m (3 ft.) in height and 60 cm (2 ft.) in width. The new red foliage and glossy dark green mature foliage are only rarely bothered by black spot.

WINTER PROTECTION: Full protection required. Easy rose to grow.

COMMENTS: "Very pretty. Not a great producer." "This rose is a good garden rose, but not especially suited for a show rose."

Royal William (Fragrant Charm, Duftzauber) — *Hybrid Tea*

FLOWER: 'Royal William' produces large, dark red, high centered blooms on individual long stems. It is a very productive rose that blooms in flushes with only a short break between.

FRAGRANCE: Faint to moderate.

FORM & FOLIAGE: This is a sturdy bush that grows about 1 m (3 ft.) in height and 60 cm (2 ft.) in width. When grown in full sun, the foliage is glossy and only occasionally gets mildew or black spot.

WINTER PROTECTION: Full protection required. Easy rose to grow.

COMMENTS: "Gorgeous red blooms." 'Royal William' commemorates the arrival of King William III in England in 1688." It frequently wins ribbons at the Calgary Rose Show.

Scentimental

Floribunda

FLOWER: Every bloom on 'Scentimental' is different. They are red and white striped, but classified as a red blend. Sometimes a plant will produce a nearly white bloom right beside a nearly red bloom. Blooms are cupped, double, and medium sized. Most blooms are produced in small clusters. There are 3 to 4 flushes per summer.

FRAGRANCE: Moderate.

FORM & FOLIAGE: 'Scentimental' is a bushy plant that produces an abundance of canes and lots of glossy foliage, forming a thick rounded plant about 1 m (3 ft.) in height and 75 cm (2.5 ft.) in width. It has good disease resistance, but should be planted where there is good air circulation to help it avoid powdery mildew. It can handle some shade, but produces fewer blooms. It will sometimes grow more foliage than flowers.

WINTER PROTECTION: Full protection required. Easy to average rose to grow.

COMMENTS: "A nice rose with pleasant fragrance. Grows very bushy." "Love this one."

Secret

Hybrid Tea

FLOWER: Medium to large blossoms are white edged with the most delicate pink and are officially classified as a pink blend. The blooms on 'Secret' are usually beautifully high centered, but sometimes they are more cup shaped. Early in the season, most of the blooms are one to a stem, but later in the summer clusters of 3 to 5 flowers predominate. Bloom production is prolific. Rain will cause the flowers to spot.

FRAGRANCE: Strong.

FORM & FOLIAGE: 'Secret' grows as bushy plants to about 1 m (3 ft.) in height and 75 cm (2.5 ft.) in width. Its foliage is glossy and abundant, but prone to mildew and black spot, especially if crowded or in an area of poor air circulation. Also, aphids love 'Secret'.

WINTER PROTECTION: Full protection required. Average rose to grow.

COMMENTS: "Blooms in 3 long flushes. One of our favourites. Love to cut these to give to people." "Sweet fragrance. Grows well on the south side of the house." One of the most fragrant Hybrid Teas.

Sexy Rexy

Floribunda

FLOWER: When 'Sexy Rexy' blooms, it produces a huge number of medium pink, double blooms in small clusters all over the plant. There is a great flush of blooms in early summer and then it takes a break before producing another large flush of blooms in the late summer. Blooms keep their colour and stay on the plant a long time.

FRAGRANCE: None to very faint.

FORM & FOLIAGE: 'Sexy Rexy' has glossy foliage with good disease resistance. The plants are moderately bushy and grow to about 75 cm (2.5 ft.) in height and 60 cm (2 ft.) in width.

WINTER PROTECTION: Full protection required. Easy rose to grow.

COMMENTS: "Everyone needs this rose in their garden. A mass of blooms." "My favorite Floribunda, and not because it is named after a male stripper—it just blooms and blooms." 'Sexy Rexy' has won the best Floribunda Spray trophy 4 times at the Calgary Rose Show.

Sheila's Perfume
Floribunda

FLOWER: 'Sheila's Perfume' produces yellow blend, medium sized, semi-double blooms with a classic high center. The flower production is very good with fragrant blooms in small clusters all over the plant.

FRAGRANCE: Very strong.

FORM & FOLIAGE: The plant will grow tall and narrow, up to 1.1 m (3.5 ft.) in height and 75 cm (2.5 ft.) in width. It likes lots of sun and the glossy foliage is very disease resistant.

WINTER PROTECTION: Full protection required. Easy rose to grow.

COMMENTS: "Great rose." "Great bloomer. Wonderful scent." "Our rose is 8 years old and has done fairly well over the years. It continues to produce a lot of blooms each year."

Sunset Boulevard
Floribunda

FLOWER: 'Sunset Boulevard' has small clusters of medium sized, orange pink blooms with high centres in flushes through the summer. The flower production of this rose is very good. The blooms do fade a little as they age.

FRAGRANCE: Moderate.

FORM & FOLIAGE: A small plant, only about 60 cm (2 ft.) in height and width, 'Sunset Boulevard' blooms well and is very attractive even with partial shade. The glossy foliage is immune to all of the common rose maladies.

WINTER PROTECTION: Full protection required. Easy rose to grow.

COMMENTS: "Not too large a plant. Rapid flower repeats. Gets only morning sun, but still does well." "Pretty, unusual colouring."

Sunsprite
Floribunda

FLOWER: The medium sized blooms on 'Sunsprite' are rich, bright, deep yellow and do not fade. Flower production is in flushes but the flushes tend to run together so that the plant nearly always has one or two flowers on it. If there is a prolonged period of wet weather, the rain can sometimes cause the flowers to ball and not open properly, but this is a rare problem in Calgary.

FRAGRANCE: Beautiful, strong licorice scent.

FORM & FOLIAGE: A tough, healthy plant with glossy foliage, 'Sunsprite' likes the sun and will do well on the south side of a house. It will grow to about 75 cm (2.5 ft.) in height and width.

WINTER PROTECTION: Full protection required. Average rose to grow.

COMMENTS: "'Sunsprite' is a very bright, strong yellow which holds its colour." "Great colour and blooms last a long time." Some gardeners are impressed with the flower production of 'Sunsprite' while others report it as not especially floriferous.

Sweet Chariot
Miniature

FLOWER: 'Sweet Chariot' has small double pompom flowers in large and small clusters of mauve, lavender and all intermediate shades. Flowering begins a little later than most other roses, but once it starts the plant is never out of bloom until fall frost ends the show. Rain will beat the petals off the older blooms, but there are so many that it is not a problem.

FRAGRANCE: Strong.

FORM & FOLIAGE: 'Sweet Chariot' is larger than most miniature roses. The stems are up to 45 cm (18 in.) in length and often end up drooping, especially when they are topped with very large clusters of blooms. Its foliage is matte green and resistant to almost everything. This is a good candidate for a hanging basket.

WINTER PROTECTION: Full protection required. Average to difficult rose to grow.

COMMENTS: "At a little distance, the plant provides a splash of colour, but up close it is the fragrance that draws the attention." "The blooms will burn if the sun is too hot or if the plant becomes too dry. Midday shade is appreciated." "Love the fragrance."

Sweet Fairy
Micro Miniature

FLOWER: The small clusters of tiny 1 cm (0.5 in.) pompoms of light pink are in perfect proportion to the tiny foliage and rounded shape of the plant. Rain will knock the petals off the older blooms. Blooming is in flushes with a quick repeat.

FRAGRANCE: Strong.

FORM & FOLIAGE: 'Sweet Fairy' is a small, rounded plant with tiny foliage and neat even growth. The glossy foliage seems to be immune to all of the normal rose diseases. It will grow to about 15 cm (6 in.) in height.

WINTER PROTECTION: Full protection required. Easy rose to grow.

COMMENTS: "Lovely fragrance on a tiny little rose." "Blooms well in a sunny window in the house and the fragrance is so welcome in the middle of winter but watch out for spider mites." The Calgary Rose Society sells a large number of 'Sweet Fairy' roses each spring by encouraging people to "smell the little pink rose."

The Fairy
Polyantha

FLOWER: Abundant, small, light pink blooms cover 'The Fairy' in a nearly continuous show from midsummer to fall. The rosette shaped flowers are fully double and start out cupped, then open flat, but it is the mass effect that impresses.

FRAGRANCE: None to faint.

FORM & FOLIAGE: 'The Fairy' is a ground cover rose that grows about 30 cm (1 ft.) in height and 60 cm (2 ft.) in width. The plant has pale glossy leaves and a naturally spreading habit. It is usually disease resistant, but can occasionally get black spot.

WINTER PROTECTION: Semi-hardy. Some winter protection required. Easy rose to grow.

COMMENTS: "Best Polyantha in my collection." "Winterize, even though it is tough as nails. Every garden has a corner for this little Polyantha." "To get it to do its best, fertilize regularly."

Tiffany

Hybrid Tea

FLOWER: 'Tiffany' has large, high centered, pink blend blooms on individual stems. The bloom repeat is fast and it appears to be almost continually in bloom.

FRAGRANCE: Moderate.

FORM & FOLIAGE: 'Tiffany' produces a tall, narrow bush growing to 1 m (3 ft.) in height and 30 cm (1 ft.) in width. The glossy foliage is somewhat susceptible to mildew.

WINTER PROTECTION: Full protection required. Average rose to grow.

COMMENTS: "Very good rose, strong, with good fragrance. Elegant, long lasting blooms." 'Tiffany' has won an international award for fragrance.

Touch of Class

Hybrid Tea

FLOWER: Large, double, high center, orange pink blooms occur usually on individual stems. Flower production is very good and blooms are often 10 to 12 cm (4 to 5 in.) in diameter.

FRAGRANCE: Faint to moderate.

FORM & FOLIAGE: 'Touch of Class' has glossy, disease resistant foliage on a sturdy bush that can grow up to 1.2 m (4 ft.) in height and 1 m (3 ft.) in width. Occasionally 'Touch of Class' will get a little black spot.

WINTER PROTECTION: Full protection required. Average to difficult rose to grow.

COMMENTS: "I love the foliage. Stands up well even as a leafed shrub. Strong stems, red in colour when new. Two very nice flushes of blooms per year." "Flowers last forever even in the house. Will not open any further if cut as a bud."

Tournament of Roses

Grandiflora

FLOWER: The medium to large size blooms are classified as medium pink, but are really two tone pink, lighter on the inside and darker on the reverse of the petals. Blooms occur in small to large clusters and stay attractive on the plants for a long time. Blooming is prolific and individual blooms are double with a nice high center.

FRAGRANCE: Faint to moderate.

FORM & FOLIAGE: Plants are relatively small, up to 75 cm (2.5 ft.) in height and 60 cm (2 ft.) in width, but bushy with glossy, medium green foliage. The branches are strong enough to hold the large numbers of flowers. It likes all the sun it can get and is not affected by any of the common diseases but occasionally it hosts a colony of aphids.

WINTER PROTECTION: Full protection required. Easy rose to grow.

COMMENTS: "Beautiful form and texture." "Very showy in the garden. Viewer's favourite." "Occasionally throws a huge spray that is just incredible." "Love this one. Flowers last a long time. One of my favourites."

Trumpeter
Floribunda

FLOWER: 'Trumpeter' in full bloom is one of the most colourful sights in the Calgary rose world. The bright, orange red blooms seem to cover the whole plant. Each medium sized, double bloom has about 39 petals with wavy edges and an open cupped shape. The blooms are in small and large clusters that are heavy enough to bow down the branches, especially when it rains. Bloom clusters last a long time and gradually fade.

FRAGRANCE: None to faint.

FORM & FOLIAGE: 'Trumpeter' grows as wide as it does tall because the weight of the flower sprays bends the branches down. Even if the branches are staked for support, it will grow no more than 60 to 75 cm (2 to 2.5 ft.) in height. It is not troubled by mildew, but can get a little late season black spot. Aphids find it attractive.

WINTER PROTECTION: Full protection required. Easy rose to grow.

COMMENTS: "Gorgeous." "One of my first roses—I love it!" "'Trumpeter' in full bloom is astonishing. I have a photo in which I can count 34 blooms on one plant." "This rose is rated by Peter Harkness (England) as being close to the perfect rose."

Victor Borge
Hybrid Tea

FLOWER: 'Victor Borge' produces high centred flowers, on single cutting stems, that are medium orange, apricot, or peach on the tops of the petals and a lighter yellow orange on the reverse of the petals. Depending on growing conditions, the blooms can be medium sized to very large. Flower production is modest, but the plants are nearly always in bloom.

FRAGRANCE: Faint to moderate.

FORM & FOLIAGE: This rose grows to 75 cm (2.5 ft.) in height and 60 cm (2 ft.) in width. 'Victor Borge' prefers lots of sun and has good disease resistance.

WINTER PROTECTION: Full protection required. Average rose to grow.

COMMENTS: "Love the colour. Each petal folds back upon itself as the bloom opens wide to display the bright yellow stamens. 'Victor Borge' produces large splashes of colour in the garden."

Warm Wishes (Sunset Celebration)
Hybrid Tea

FLOWER: The apricot or orange pink blooms of medium to large size grow as singles or small clusters. The blooms are high centred and 'Warm Wishes' repeats well.

FRAGRANCE: Faint.

FORM & FOLIAGE: 'Warm Wishes' is an upright, bushy plant that will grow to 1.2 m (4 ft.) in height and 60 cm (2 ft.) in width. Its foliage is medium green, semi-glossy and quite disease resistant. This rose prefers full sun.

WINTER PROTECTION: Full protection required. Average rose to grow.

COMMENTS: "Mild, fruity scent." "Beautiful colour." "My favourite. Flowers retain their colour and are long lasting. A healthy plant with nice foliage. Flowers are great for cutting."

TENDER ROSE CHECKLIST: PERSONAL FAVOURITES

16 Award-Winning Roses

MANY ROSARIANS IN CALGARY GROW some roses with the hopes of taking home ribbons and trophies at the annual Rose Show. The winning roses are considered to be the best rose in that category that year and provide bragging rights. With the idea that you might want to add some of these award-winning roses to your garden, we've included lists of the winning roses in some of the major trophy categories since inception of the trophy. If there is no rose listed, then the trophy was not awarded in that particular year.

The roses listed in the following tables are colour coded to enable you to quickly search for winning roses in your favourite colours to add to your garden. Rose names followed by an asterisk* are illustrated and described in one or the other of the preceding chapters *Favourite Hardy Roses* or *Favourite Tender Roses*. Some rose names are in white type to improve their legibility against a dark background.

Canadian and American Rose Society Rose Colour Classification

	white, near white, & white blend
	light yellow
	medium yellow
	deep yellow
	yellow blend
	apricot & apricot blend
	orange & orange blend
	orange-pink & orange-pink blend
	orange-red & orange-red blend
	light pink
	medium pink
	deep pink
	pink blend
	medium red
	dark red
	red blend
	mauve & mauve blend
	russet/brown

	Queen of Show Best Hybrid Tea (Single Rose)	Queen of Show Next Best Hybrid Tea (Single Rose)	Best Pink Hybrid Tea (Single Bloom)	Best White Hybrid Tea (Single Bloom)
1974	Pascali*	–	–	–
1975	Pascali*	–	–	–
1976	Alec's Red	–	–	–
1977	Tropicana	–	–	–
1978	Peace*	–	–	–
1979	Pascali*	–	–	–
1980	Pristine*	–	–	–
1981	Dickson's Flame	–	–	–
1982	Chicago Peace	–	–	–
1983	Pascali*	–	–	–
1984	Tropicana	–	–	–
1985	Die Welt (The World)	–	–	–
1986	Futura	–	–	–
1987	Ingrid Bergman	Duftzauber	Criterion	
1988	Paradise	Double Delight*	Silver Jubilee	–
1989	Peter Frankenfeld	Kordes Perfecta	Peter Frankenfeld	–
1990	Paradise	Pascali*	All American Beauty*	–
1991	Olympiad*	Touch of Class*	Electron*	–
1992	Perfect Moment	National Trust	Electron*	–
1993	Loving Memory	Brigadoon	Peter Frankenfeld	–
1994	Papa Meilland	Polarstern	Electron*	–
1995	Precious Platinum	Golden Splendor	Capt. Harry Stebbings	Sheer Bliss
1996	Red Devil	Headliner	Headliner	Garden Party*
1997	Electron*	–	Silver Jubilee	Pascali*
1998	Double Delight*	–	–	–
1999	Royal Highness	Olympic Medalist	Royal Highness	French Lace
2000	Polarstern	Ave Marie	Ave Marie	Polarstern
2001	Electron*	Ave Marie	Bewitched	Polarstern
2002	Schwarze Madonna	Olympiad*	Marijke Koopman*	Pristine*
2003	Folklore*	Schwarze Madonna	Electron*	Pascali*
2004	Pristine*	Schwarze Madonna	Marijke Koopman*	Pristine*
2005	Chicago Peace	Double Delight*	Pink Peace	Suffolk
2006	Pristine*	Marilyn Monroe*	Truly Yours	Pristine*
2007	Michelangelo	Canadian Sunset	Gemini	Princesse de Monaco
2008	Elina	Folklore*	Gemini	Sheer Bliss
2009	Big Purple*	Valencia	Dainty Bess	Sheer Bliss
2010	Valencia	Gemini	Gemini	Moonstone

	Best Hybrid Tea (Spray)	Best Floribunda (Spray)	Best Grandiflora (Spray)	Best English Rose
1974	–	–	Camelot	–
1975	–	Europeana*	Queen Elizabeth*	–
1976	–	–	–	–
1977	–	Iceberg*	Carousel	
1978	–	–	–	–
1979	–	–	–	
1980	–	Europeana*	Queen Elizabeth*	–
1981	–	Europeana*	Camelot	
1982		–	–	–
1983	Kordes Perfecta	Fire King	Camelot	–
1984	La Minuette	City of Leeds	Camelot	
1985	Fragrant Cloud*	Europeana*	–	
1986	Olympiad*	Fire Chief	Queen Elizabeth*	–
1987	Double Delight*	Europeana*	Camelot	
1988	Honor	Europeana*	Pink Parfait*	–
1989	Olympiad*	Europeana*	–	–
1990	Flaming Peace	Iceberg*	Gold Medal*	–
1991	Smokey	Sexy Rexy*	Gold Medal*	
1992	–	Sexy Rexy*	Tournament of Roses*	–
1993	Folklore*	Montana	Pink Parfait*	–
1994	–	Simplicity	–	–
1995	Karl Herbst	–	Gold Medal*	–
1996	–	Impatient	–	–
1997	Ave Marie	Europeana*	–	–
1998		–	–	
1999	Paul Shirville	Iceberg*	–	
2000	–	Sexy Rexy*	Waiheke	–
2001	–	Impatient	–	
2002	Tequila Sunrise	Impatient	–	
2003	Stephens' Big Purple*	Tabris	Tournament of Roses*	L.D. Braithwaite*
2004	First Prize*	Sexy Rexy*	Tournament of Roses*	Golden Celebration
2005	Secret*	Chihuly	Cherry Parfait*	Golden Celebration
2006	–	–	Cherry Parfait*	L.D. Braithwaite*
2007	Berolina	English Miss*	Cherry Parfait*	Graham Thomas*
2008	Royal William*	Glad Tidings	–	Prospero
2009	–	Iceberg*	Wild Blue Yonder	Mary Rose*
2010	–	Playboy*	White Lightnin'	Lillian Austin

	Best Miniature (Single Bloom)	Best Miniature (Spray)	Best Shrub (Spray)	Most Fragrant Rose
1974	–	–	–	–
1975	–	–	–	–
1976	–	–	–	–
1977	–	–	–	–
1978	–	–	–	–
1979	–	–	–	–
1980	–	–	–	–
1981	Beauty Secret	Pixie Rose		
1982	Pacesetter	Dwarf King	–	–
1983	Cinderella	Mary Marshall	Morden Cardinette	–
1984	Pacesetter	Scarlet Gem	Adelaide Hoodless*	
1985	Pacesetter	Beauty Secret	Adelaide Hoodless*	
1986	Young Cale	Beauty Secret	Pink Grootendorst*	
1987	Snow Bride	Cupcake	Red Grootendorst	
1988	Charmglo	Scarlet Gem	Thérèse Bugnet*	
1989	Holy Toledo	Cupcake	Adelaide Hoodless*	
1990	Pacesetter	Starina	Adelaide Hoodless*	
1991	Snow Bride	Winsome	Adelaide Hoodless*	
1992	Living Bouquet	Baby Katie	Bonica*	–
1993	Red Beauty	Stacey Sue	Bonica*	–
1994	Radiant	–	Meidomonac	
1995	Minnie Pearl*	Bon Homme	Bonica*	–
1996	Cupcake	–	Morden Centennial	–
1997	Toy Clown	Popcorn	Bonica*	
1998	–	–	–	–
1999	Blue Ice	My Valentine	Jens Munk	Heirloom
2000	Loving Touch	–	Adelaide Hoodless*	Fragrant Cloud*
2001	Pierrine	Sincerely Yours	Carefree Delight	Sharifa Asma
2002	Pierrine	Young Cale	Prairie Joy	Fragrant Cloud*
2003	Tropical Twist	Lemon Delight	Prairie Star	Thérèse Bugnet*
2004	X-Rated	Young Cale	Hope for Humanity*	Blue Girl
2005	Kristen	Kordes Orange	Robusta*	Fragrant Cloud*
2006	Sun Sprinkles	Jean Kenneally	Linda Campbell	Fragrant Cloud*
2007	X-Rated	Hi Ho	Adelaide Hoodless*	Secret*
2008	Lights of Broadway	Ruby Rambler	Hope for Humanity*	Barbra Streisand*
2009	Miss Flippins	Jeanne Lajoie*	Winnipeg Parks*	Double Delight*
2010	X-Rated	Playgold	John Davis*	Neptune

A

Acid soil: Soil that has a pH of less than 7.0. Roses prefer pH between 6.0 and 6.5.

Alkaline soil: Soil with a pH higher than 7.0. Calgary's soil is alkaline (pH = 7.7).

Anther: In the flower, the upper part of the stamen which holds the pollen.

Aoûter: French word indicating how rose wood begins to prepare for cold weather.

Armed: A plant bearing strong thorns.

Axil: The angle between the upper side of a leaf and a stem where an auxiliary bud develops.

Auxiliary bud: A bud that develops in the axil of a leaf of a plant. Auxiliary buds develop from nodes that then become new stems.

B

Balling: The clinging together of petals in wet weather so that the bloom fails to open.

Bare root: A dormant, pruned plant that is sold without soil.

Basal breaks: New canes sprouting from the bud union on a grafted rose.

Bi-coloured: A flower that has two different shades of colour, often sharply contrasting.

Black spot: A fungal disease that affects leaves and stems of roses, causing black spots to appear.

Bleeding: The loss of sap from plant tissues due to late pruning.

Blind shoot: A mature stem which fails to produce a flower due to frost damage, lack of nutrients, shortage of light or tiny midges. Cutting the cane back to a healthy bud will produce a flowering shoot.

Blown bloom: A many-petalled bloom that has opened wide, revealing its stamens.

Boss: The cluster of stamens at the flower centre.

Bract: A leaf that looks like a green petal and serves to protect the opening bud.

Bud: There are two types of buds on a rose bush. A flower bud is an unopened flower. A growth bud is the beginning stage of a shoot.

Budeye: The point where a leaf is attached to a cane. Other than basal breaks emerging directly from the bud union, budeyes are the only points from which a new cane will grow. Pruning canes at a 45° angle just above a budeye will encourage new growth.

Bud union: The point where the named cultivar joins the understock or rootstock. The swollen area, at the top of the shank, from which new canes (basal breaks) emerge.

Burning: The bleaching or scorching of rose petals due to sunburn or over fertilization.

Button eye: A condition found in the centre of some rose blooms where the petals are folded inwards to form a 'button' (e.g. 'Madame Hardy').

C

Calyx: The group of tough, outer, green petals that protects the bud before it opens. Individually these petals are called sepals.

Cane: A supportive branch of a rose bush. Canes differ from stems in that they have hardened and are thicker.

Canker: A disease caused by fungi that produce brown, oval shaped, sunken or shrivelled areas anywhere on the cane.

Chinook: A dry, warm, down slope wind that occurs in the lee of a mountain range. Calgary experiences between 5 and 15 Chinooks each winter, each lasting between 1 and 5 days and usually raising the temperature to above freezing.

Chlorosis: An abnormal yellowing or blanching of the leaves due to lack of chlorophyll.

Confused centre: Occurs when the petals in the centre of a bloom are disarranged, giving an asymmetrical appearance.

Cross: The offspring arising from cross-pollination.

Crown: The point where roots and stems join.

Cultivar: The horticultural term for a "cultivated variety" meaning a plant specially bred and not occurring naturally in the wild. Most of the rose plants in our gardens are cultivars.

Cutting: A piece cut from a stem that is used for propagation.

D

Deadheading: Removal of the spent blooms. It is usually recommended to make the cut just above a 5-leaflet set.

Dieback: The progressive dying back of a shoot from its tip.

Diploid: Plants that have two sets of chromosomes.

Disbudding: Removing buds to encourage fewer but larger blooms.

Dormant period: The time when the plant has naturally stopped growing due to low temperatures and shorter days.

Dormant spray: A chemical solution, usually Horticulture Oil and Lime Sulphur, sprayed on plants before winter or before buds appear in spring to kill fungal spores and insect eggs.

Double: A flower that has many rows of petals. Double rose flowers are divided into three categories: semi-double (10 – 20 petals), double (20 – 40 petals), and very double (over 40 petals).

E

English rose: The name used to describe roses bred in England by David Austin.

Explorer rose: A series of super-hardy roses bred by the Canadian Department of Agriculture to survive the Canadian winter.

Exudates: Any fluid that filters from the circulatory system. In plants, root exudates aid in nutrition uptake, healing and defence.

F

Fasciation: Abnormal growth occurring in flowers and stems of plants that spreads laterally, resulting in flattened, band-like growth. Can be caused by spontaneous cell mutation, certain pathogens, or damage to a growing tip.

Filament: The lower part of a stamen, which joins it to the anther.

Floriferous: Literally, having flowers. In common usage the term is used to describe a plant with an abundance of flowers.

Flush: The period during which the plant bears its normal complement of blooms.

Foliar feed: A fertilizer capable of being sprayed on and absorbed by the leaves.

Fragrance: The scent or smell of a flower coming from oil evaporating from cells at the base of the petals. Some roses have fragrance from their leaves.

Full blown: A mature, open bloom showing stamens.

Fungicide: A chemical used to control diseases caused by fungi.

Fungus: A primitive form of plant life that is the most common cause of disease in roses.

G

Grading: Classification of rose bushes according to the number and size of stems: grade 1, excellent; grade 1½, good; grade 2, poor.

Grafting: The process of joining a stem or bud of one plant to the stem of another in order to produce a more vigorous plant.

Grooming: Physical improvement of a specimen by an exhibitor prior to entry in the Rose Show.

Guard petals: The outermost petals on a rose that protect the flower bud.

H

Habit: The characteristic growth or general appearance of a rose, varying from compact or rigid, to spreading or arching.

Harden off: 1. The process of suspending the general fertilizing of a rose—in the autumn—to allow the plant to prepare for winter. 2. The process of gradually exposing a plant to longer and longer periods outside before planting.

Hardwood cutting: A cutting taken from ripe wood and used for propagation.

Hardy: A plant that will withstand Calgary's winters without any protection and bloom the next summer.

Heeling in: Temporary planting of roses in a trench until suitable weather conditions allow permanent planting.

High-centred bud: Long, conical-shaped buds, typically associated with Hybrid Tea roses.

Hips: The seed bearing fruit of the rose formed when it is pollinated. Hips are red to orange but may be dark purple to black in some species.

Honeydew: The sticky, sugary secretion deposited on plant leaves and stems by aphids.

Hybrid: The plant that results when two different varieties or species are crossed.

Hybridize: To create a new rose cultivar by selectively fertilizing one rose with the pollen of another one in the hopes that the progeny will carry some of the traits of each.

I

Imbricated: Blossom petals that neatly overlap.

Incurved: Blossom petals that curve inwards to form a compact, rounded shape.

Inflorescence: The general arrangement of flowers on an axis. An inflorescence may consist of one spray or a number of sprays.

Inorganic: A chemical or fertilizer that is not obtained from a plant or animal source.

Insecticide: A chemical used to control insect pests.

Internode: The section of a stem between two nodes.

L

Larva: An immature, wingless, wormlike creature hatched from an egg, that goes through minor changes to form a pupa.

Leaflet: A part of a compound leaf. It may resemble an entire leaf but is not born on a stem as a leaf is, but rather on a vein of the whole leaf.

Lateral bud: A bud located on the side of a shoot rather than at the terminal end.

Leaching: The removal of chemicals from the soil by rain or watering.

M

Macronutrient: A chemical that is needed in large amounts by a plant to stimulate growth.

Micronutrient: A chemical that is only needed in small amounts by a plant.

Mulch: An organic material, such as compost, rotted manure, grass clippings or shredded leaves which protects the plant from weeds, water evaporation and changes in soil temperature. It enriches and improves the texture and structure of the soil.

N

Node: The point at which a leaf or side shoot joins a stem.

O

Old Garden roses: Cultivated roses that existed prior to 1867. Most bloom only once and are very fragrant.

Once-blooming: A rose that has one annual flush of blooms. Most species and many Old Garden roses are once-blooming. Most modern roses are repeat bloomers.

Organic: A chemical or fertilizer that is obtained from a plant or animal source.

Ovary: The reproductive part of the flower that contains the ovules.

Ovule: The part of the female organ of the flower that turns into a seed after fertilization.

Own-root: A rose that is grown directly on its own roots rather than by grafting onto a rootstock. In severe winter areas, own-root roses offer the advantage of being able to regenerate, true-to-name, directly from their roots.

P

Pedicel: The part of the stem between the flower and the uppermost leaf.

Pegging: The bending over of long shoots by means of pegs to encourage extra flowering laterals from the nodes along the stem.

pH: A measure of acidity and alkalinity. Substances with a pH below 7.0 are acidic, those with a pH above 7.0 are alkaline. Roses like soil with a pH between 6.0 and 6.5.

Pistil: The female organ of a flower, comprised of the stigma, style and ovary.

Pith: The spongy material at the centre of the stem.

Pollen: The yellow dust produced by the anthers. Pollen contains the sperm that fertilizes the egg within the ovary to produce a seed.

Pollination: The application of pollen to the stigma of a flower.

Powdery mildew: A fungal disease affecting roses which causes a white powder to appear on leaves, stems and buds.

Pruning: The removal of parts of the plant in order to improve its appearance and performance.

Pupa: A life stage of some insects that undergo complete transformation. The life stages of these insects are: embryo, larva, pupa and adulthood.

Q

Quartered: Flowers, especially those of old rose cultivars, that are roughly divided into quarters when open.

R

Rambler: A vigorous climbing rose with a loose, lax arrangement of stems.

Recurrent: Repeat flowering.

Reflexed: Flower petals whose edges are turned back away from the centre of the flower.

Remontant: Flowering more than once during the growing season.

Reverse: The side of the petal that faces away from the centre.

Reversion: Either a sport which returns to the colour or growth habit of its parent or a cultivar that is overgrown by suckers arising from the rootstock.

Rootstock: A rose whose vigorous roots are used as the foundation for a grafted rose. The use of rootstocks allows varieties that would not grow well on their own roots to be propagated commercially.

Rosa: The genus to which all roses belong.

S

Seedling: A young plant grown from seed.

Semi-double: A rose blossom with 10 to 20 petals.

Semi-hardy: Roses that require partial winter protection in Calgary.

Sepal: One of the five green divisions of the calyx.

Shovel pruning: Digging up and discarding an unwanted plant.

Single: A rose blossom with 5 to 9 petals arranged in one layer around a central cluster of stamens.

Softwood cutting: New growth that is flexible and not fully mature, usually with leaves attached.

Species: A wild-growing plant where every individual of that plant has the same appearance and genetic makeup. Seeds raised from the plant will produce more plants virtually identical to the parent.

Sport: A spontaneous mutation in growth habit or flower character. Some climbing roses are sports of bush roses. Some sports are stable and can lead to the introduction of a new rose. Others will quickly revert back to the parent.

Spotting: The appearance of spots and blemishes on the petals caused by wet weather. Most frequently seen on light coloured roses.

Spray: A group of blooms on a single stem.

Stamen: The male portion of a flower's reproductive system, comprised of a filament and an anther (pollen pad).

Standard: A standard tree rose is formed by grafting a desirable cultivar, that forms the head, on a tall stem.

Stigma: The female portion of the flower that receives pollen grains for fertilization.

Stipule: The small outgrowth at the base of the leafstalk.

Stratification: The breaking of seed dormancy by placing hips in a refrigerator or overwintering them outdoors.

Style: The centre part of a pistil between the stigma and the ovary.

Sucker: Offsets from the original rose. Suckers can spring up at some distance from the roots of an established rose. If dug up, a sucker root will appear as a creamy white underground branch, sometimes with fine feeder roots. These are excellent for starting new roses. If the sucker springs from the grafted understock, the sucker will be of a different variety than the original rose.

Systemic: A pesticide or fungicide that goes inside the plant and travels in the sap stream.

Tetraploid: Plants having four sets of chromosomes.

T

Triploid: Plants that have three sets of chromosomes. Triploid roses tend not to produce hips.

V

Variety: A plant that originates naturally in the wild without human intervention. It constitutes a subgroup within a species. Any distinct type of rose which bears one or more unique features. Almost everyone uses the term to mean any plant distinctly different from another plant whether bred or occurring naturally in the wild.

W

Winterkill: Death of all or part of a rose because of winter conditions.

18 *Appendix*

Selected Bibliography

American Rose Society (2010). *Handbook for selecting roses – Annual.* Shreveport, LA: American Rose Society. Available from <**www.ars.org**/> and <**www. calgaryrosesociety.ca**>

Beales, P., Cairns, T., Duncan, W., Fagan, G., Grant, W., Grapes, K., Harkness, P., Hughes, K., Mattock, J. & Ruston, D. (1999). *Botanica's roses: The encyclopedia of roses.* Vancouver, BC: Raincoast Books.

Beales, P. (2004). *A passion for roses.* London, UK: Mitchell Beazley.

Calgary Rose Society (ND). *Rose round-up: Newsletter of the Calgary Rose Society.* Published 6 times per year. Available as a member of the CRS. Available from <**www.calgaryrosesociety.ca**>

Canadian Rose Society (2007). *Colour classification of garden roses.* Kingston, ON: Canadian Rose Society. Available from <**www.canadianrosesociety.org**>

Hole, L. (1997), *Lois Hole's rose favourites.* Edmonton, AB: Lone Pine Publishing.

Krussmann, G. (1981). *The complete book of roses.* Portland, OR: Timber Press.

Porter, B.J. & Pittao, A.F. (2008). *Growing roses in Saskatchewan.* Lloydminster, SK: Saskatchewan Rose Society. Available from <**www.icangarden.com/ uploaddocuments/d2505+SRS%20General%20Brochure%200508.PDF**>

Quest-Ritson, C. & Quest-Ritson, B. (2003). *Encyclopedia of roses: The definitive A–Z guide.* Toronto, ON: Dorling Kindersley Limited/Tourmaline Editions Inc.

Richer, C. & Davidson, C.G. (2004). *Winter-hardy roses: Explorer, Parkland and Prairie series.* Ottawa, ON: Agriculture & Agri-Food Canada. Available from <**www.canadianrosesociety.org**>

Shewchuk, G.W. (1999). *Roses: A gardener's guide for the plains and prairies.* Edmonton, AB: University of Alberta Press.

Svejda, F. (2008). *The Canadian Explorer roses.* London, ON: National-Roses-Canada. Available from <**www.rosescanada.ca**/>

Societies and Organizations

- Alberta Horticulture Society, <**www.icangarden.com/clubs/AHA**>
- American Rose Society (ARS), <**www.ars.org**>
- Calgary Rose Society (CRS), <**www.calgaryrosesociety.ca**>
- Calgary Horticultural Society, <**calhort.org/home**>
- Canadian Rose Society, <**www.canadianrosesociety.org**>
- National Roses Canada, <**www.rosescanada.ca**>

Sources for Purchasing Roses

- **Golden Acre Garden Centre**
  620 Goddard Avenue NE, Calgary, Alberta T2K 5X3
  Phone: (403) 274•4286
  Fax: (403) 275•5615
  Hours: Monday – Sunday 8:00 am – 9:00 pm
  Website: <**www.goldenacre.ca/new_design**>

- **Greengate Garden Centre Ltd.**
  14111 Macleod Trail S., Calgary, Alberta T2Y 1M6
  Phone: (403) 256•1212
  Fax: (403) 256•4420
  Hours: Monday – Sunday 9:00 am – 9:00 pm
  Website: <**www.greengate.ca**>

- **Greenland Garden Centre**
  23108 Highway 16, Sherwood Park, Alberta T8A 4V2
  Phone: (780) 467•7557
  Fax: (780) 467•8940
  Hours: Monday – Friday 10:00 am – 6:00 pm
  Saturday 9:00 am – 5:00 pm
  Sunday & Holidays: 12:00 am – 5:00 pm
  Website: <**www.greenlandgarden.com**>

- **Hole's Greenhouses and Gardens**
  101 Bellerose Drive, St. Albert, Alberta T8N 8N8
  Phone: (780) 419•6800
  Toll-Free Phone: 1 (888) 884•6537
  Fax: (780) 459•6042
  Toll-Free Fax: 1 (888) 465•3732
  Hours: Monday – Friday 9:00 am – 7:00 pm
  Saturday & Sunday 9:00 am – 4:00 pm
  Website: <**www.holesonline.com**>

- **Sunnyside Home & Garden Centre**
  3439 – 69 Street NW, Calgary, Alberta T3B 2J8
  Phone: (403) 288•3006
  Fax: (403) 286•6908
  Hours: Monday – Sunday 9:00 am – 9:00 pm
  Website: <**www.sunnysidehomeandgarden.com**>

Online

- **Pickerings, Ontario**
  Website: <**www.pickeringnurseries.com**>

- **Palatine, Ontario**
  Website: <**www.palatineroses.com**>

- **Classic Miniature Roses, British Columbia**
  Website: <**www.theheatherfarm.com**>

Viewing Roses in Calgary

- **Calgary Rose Society – Open Gardens.**
  Locations are published annually in the society's
  newsletter, the *Rose Roundup.*

- **Calgary Horticultural Society – Garden
  Competition.**
  Details of the viewing weekend for touring the
  winning gardens (usually the third weekend in
  July) are posted on the Society's website at
  <**https://www.calhort.org/events/garden
  competition.aspx**>

- **Elliston Park**
- *Address*: 1827 – 68 Street SE, Calgary, Alberta
- *Phone*: (403) 268•2489 or 311 for City of Calgary
  Information, in Calgary.
- *Description*: A mixture of roses with emphasis on
  hardy shrubs. Enter via 60th Street, to the main
  car park, and the three rose beds are located in the
  north west corner of the park, near the sundial.
- *Number of Plants*: About 200 bushes.
- *Admission*: Free.
- *Access*: 5:00 am – 11:00 pm, daily, year round.
- *Wheelchair Accessible*: Yes
- *Parking*: Free, on-site, with west lot off 60 Street
  SE and the east lot off 68 Street SE.
- *Website*: <**http://www.calgary.ca/portal/server.
  pt/gateway/PTARGS_0_0_780_247_0_43/
  http%3B/content.calgary.ca/CCA/
  City+Hall/Business+Units/Parks/
  Find+a+Park+or+Pathway/Major+Parks/
  SE+Parks/Elliston+Park+.htm**>

- **Calgary Zoo Botanical Garden & Prehistoric
  Park – Dorothy Harvie Gardens Rose
  Collection**
- *Address*: 1300 Zoo Road NE, Calgary,
  Alberta T2E 7V6
- *Phone*: (403) 232•9300
- *Description*: A mixture of most types of roses with
  an emphasis on the smaller more compact hardy
  shrubs from the Parkland, Explorer and Morden
  series.
- *Number of Plants*: About 60 bushes of 40 varieties.
- *Admission*: With Zoo Entrance. Adults: $19.00;
  Seniors (60+): $17.00; Children 3 – 12: $11.00;
  Infants 2 and under: Free.
- *Access*: Year round, daily 9:00 am – 5:00 pm, with
  gates closing at 6:00 pm.
- *Wheelchair Accessible*: Yes.
- *Parking*: Free carparks on both the north and west
  sides of the site.
- *Website*: **http://www.calgaryzoo.org/index.
  php?option=com_content&task=view&id=21&It
  emid=281**>

Viewing Roses Around Alberta

- **Crop Diversification Centre South Rose Garden**
- *Address*: 301 Horticulture Station Road East, Brooks, Alberta T1R 1R6
- *Phone*: (403) 362·1350
- *Description*: The CDSC Rose Garden contains very rare Canadian- and USA-bred hardy roses that were used in breeding by Agriculture Canada's lines of Explorer and Parkland roses. In fact, some of the roses in the garden were thought to be extinct. Both named roses and unnamed seedlings used for breeding can be found here, bred by such pioneering hybridizers as Dr. Griffith J. Buck, Georges C.J. Bugnet, Robert M. Erskine, Professor N.E. Hansen, Henry H. Marshall, Walter Schowalter, Dr. Frank L. Skinner, George Wallace, and Percy H. Wright.
- *Number of Plants*: 100+ bushes
- *Admission*: Free
- *Access*: Year round, daily, dawn till dusk with the best weeks for viewing rose blooms, generally speaking, from mid-June through the end of July.
- *Wheelchair Accessible*: Yes.
- *Parking*: Free on-site.
- *Website*: <**http://www1.agric.gov.ab.ca/ $department/deptdocs.nsf/all/opp4386**> (Scroll down this page to download the pdf file entitled *CDCS Rose Garden Guide*.)

- **The Beta Sigma Phi Rose Garden at the Devonian Botanic Gardens, University of Alberta, Faculty of Agricultural, Life and Environmental Sciences**
- *Address*: 5 kilometres north of Devon, just south of Highway 627 on Highway 60, Devon, Alberta
- *Phone*: (780) 987·3054
- *Description*: A good variety of roses in interesting groupings, but mainly Species roses and hardy shrubs.
- *Number of Plants*: 150 – 200 bushes
- *Admission*: Adults: $13.00; Seniors: $8.50; Youth 13 – 17: $5.00; Children 7 – 12: $3.00; Children under 6: Free; Student and Family concessions.
- *Access*: May 1 – October 11; May 1 – 23 and September 7 – October 11: 10:00 am – 5:00 pm daily; May 24 – September 6: 10:00 – 6: 00 pm daily, with late nights on Thursdays till 8:00 pm.
- *Wheelchair Accessible*: Yes.
- *Parking*: Free, on-site.
- *Website*: <**http://www.ales.ualberta.ca/devonian/**>

- **Camrose Rose Garden**
- *Address*: 5402 – 48 Avenue (Highway 13), Camrose, Alberta T4V 0S8
- *Phone*: (780) 672·4426
- *Description*: Found in front of the Chamber of Commerce (Bill Fowler Centre), it is a planting of a variety of hardy shrubs, Morden roses, and hybrid teas. At one time, the display included a patented variety, Camrose, developed by T&T Seeds out of Winnipeg, Manitoba.
- *Number of Plants*: About 50 bushes.
- *Admission*: Free
- *Access*: Year round, daily, dawn till dusk.
- *Wheelchair Accessible*: Yes
- *Parking*: On street, 2-hour restriction, ($1.00/hour)
- *Website*: <**http://www.camrose.ca/**>

- **Edmonton Muttart Conservatory**
- *Address*: 9626 – 96A Street, Edmonton, Alberta T6C 4L8
- *Phone*: (780) 442·3111 or 311 for City of Edmonton Information, in Edmonton.
- *Description*: A presentation of mostly hardy shrubs on the grounds of the Muttart Conservatory.
- *Number of Plants*: About 50 bushes.
- *Admission*: Conservatory: Adults (18 – 64): $10.50; Seniors (65+) and Youth (12 – 17): $8.00; Child (2 – 12): $5.25; Under 2: Free. Family, Grandparent and Multi-Facility concessions. Admission to the rose garden is free.
- *Access*: Conservatory is open year round, Monday – Friday 10:00 am – 5:00 pm; Weekends and Statutory Holidays 11:00 am – 5:00 pm; The rose garden is open year round, daily, dawn till dusk, with roses typically in bloom from mid-June through the end of July.
- *Parking*: Free.
- *Wheelchair Accessible*: Yes.
- *Website*: <**www.muttartconservatory.ca/pages/ Muttart/default.aspx**>

- **Millet Memorial Rose Garden**
- *Address*: Highway 2A, Main Street, Millet, Alberta T0C 1Z0
- *Phone*: (780) 387·5558 or (780) 387·4554 for the Town Administration.
- *Description*: Inspired by Millet resident Bernice Knight, who wanted to plant a rose in memory of her mother, the garden is maintained by *Millet in Bloom*, and consists of mostly hardy shrubs and species roses. Roses are purchased and placed in the garden in memory of a loved one. The names are indicated on a sign.
- *Number of Plants*: About 100.
- *Admission*: Free.
- *Access*: Year round, daily, dawn till dusk.
- *Wheelchair Accessible*: Yes.
- *Parking*: Free, on-street.
- *Website*: <**www.viarail.ca/jardin/en_millet-rose-garden.html**>

- **Olds College Botanic Garden**
- *Address*: 4500 – 50th Street, Olds, Alberta T4H 1R6
- *Phone*: (403) 556·8281; Toll-free: 1 (800) 661·6537
- *Description*: Revised in 2002, the garden features roses bred by Canadians, notably local Rocky Mountain House resident, Robert M. Erskine (*Prairie Peace*) and Georges C.J. Bugnet, as well as

good representations from the Parkland and Explorer series. Some Species roses and Spinosissima shrubs, and a number of other early Canadian roses are also present. The garden is to shortly feature a new rosa rugosa, developed by the owners of Brentwood Bay Nurseries, in British Columbia, named Michel Trudeau, in memory of their nephew.

- *Number of Plants*: Between 40 – 50 bushes.
- *Admission*: Free.
- *Access*: Year round, daily, dawn till dusk with the best weeks being over the summer.
- *Wheelchair Accessible*: Yes.
- *Parking*: During college term time, limited metered parking; During the summer holidays, usually ample, and free, on-site.
- *Website*: <**http://www.oldscollege.ca/botanic garden/**>

- **Red Deer City Hall Park**
- *Address*: 4914 – 48 Avenue, Red Deer, Alberta T4N 3T3
- *Phone*: (403) 342•8234 or (403) 872•2129 for the Head Gardener.
- *Description*: Dating back to 1902, the extensive garden is to be found in front of the City Hall and consists of more than sixty beds in which 35 – 37,000 annuals are planted each year, in addition to the perennials and roses. The four circular beds, where park planting zones 2, 3 and 4 meet in the centre of the garden, is where you will find the rose bushes. Some hybrid teas and hardier varieties including those from the Morden and Explorer series as well as a number of Zone 5 varieties.
- *Number of Plants*: About 70 bushes.
- *Admission*: Free.
- *Access*: year round, daily, dawn till dusk.
- *Wheelchair Accessible*: Yes.
- *Parking*: Free, on street, on the south side.
- *Website*: <**http://www.reddeer.ca/City+ Government/City+Services+and+Departments/ Recreation+Parks+and+Culture/Parks/ City+Hall+Park+Photo+Gallery/default.htm**> (There is a downloadable pdf map of the park here along with a number of photographs and a video so you can tour the park online too).

- **St. Albert Botanic Park**
- *Address*: 265 Sturgeon Road, St. Albert, Alberta T8N 1N2
- *Phone*: (780) 458•7163
- *Description*: A 37-metre, circular rose garden, established in 1995, has the nicest layout of any in Alberta. It was created to be inspirational and demonstrates the many beautiful roses that can survive the St. Albert area's harsh winters. The garden also sells a good variety of Austin, Hybrid Tea, Floribundas, Grandifloras, Modern Shrub Roses from the Parkland and Explorer series, Miniatures and Climbers on the Mother's Day weekend each year.
- *Number of Plants*: About 440 bushes of 17 varieties.
- *Access*: May 1 – August 31, daily, dawn to dusk.
- *Admission*: Free.
- *Wheelchair Accessible*: Yes.
- *Parking*: Free, on-site.
- *Website*: <**www.stalbertbotanicpark.com/**>

- **Trochu Arboretum and Gardens**
- *Address*: 622 North Road, Trochu, Alberta T0M 2C0
- *Phone*: (403) 588•8600 or (403) 442•2111
- *Description*: Roses are only a portion of an immaculate "oasis on the prairie" featuring many genera of plants.
- *Number of Plants*: About 50 bushes.
- *Access*: Victoria Day weekend in May – Thanksgiving weekend in October, daily, dawn till dusk.
- *Admission*: Suggested donation of $4.00 per person.
- *Wheelchair Accessible*: Yes.
- *Parking*: Free, on-site.
- *Website*: <**http://www.town.trochu.ab.ca/culture-tourism/trochu-arboretum-gardens/**>

- **Viking Troll Park**
- *Address*: Railway Avenue, Viking, Alberta T0B 4N0
- *Phone*: (780) 336•3466 for the Town Administration.
- *Description*: In addition to the roses, there are many other plants either native to Alberta or Scandinavia.
- *Number of Plants*: About 50 bushes.
- *Admission*: Free (but donations are welcome).
- *Access*: May to October, daily, dawn till dusk.
- *Parking*: Free, on-site.
- *Wheelchair Accessible*: Yes.
- *Website*: <**http://www.town.viking.ab.ca/**>

Abbreviations Used for Units of Measurement

- **Metric**

m	metre
cm	centimetre
mm	millimetre
l	litre
ml	millilitre
kg	kilogram
gm	gram

- **Imperial**

in.	inch
ft.	foot or feet
gal.	imperial gallon
lb.	pounds

- **Other**

tsp.	teaspoon (5 gm)
tbsp.	tablespoon (15 gm)
cup	cup (250 gm or ml)

- **Temperatures**

°C	degrees Centigrade
°F	degrees Fahrenheit

19 Index

Subject Index

Pages listed in *italics* include photographs.

Plant Index

Pages listed in *italics* include photographs.

❀ ❀ ❀

Beyond the immediate Calgary Rose Society community, we also wish to thank the following people for contributing specific photographs:

- Fred Bentler, for the Braconid Wasp (on p. 56), used by permission and found at <**http://www.bentler.us/eastern-washington/animals/insects/wasps/default. aspx**>.
- Derrick Ditchburn for the Carabid Beetle and Green Lacewing (both on p. 56), used by permission and found at <**http://www.dereilanatureinn.ca/galleries/beetles/ beetles2.htm**>.
- Dr. Rob Longair, University of Calgary, Department of Biology, for the Hover Fly (on p. 57), from his private collection, by permission.
- Dr. Joe Shorthouse, Laurentian University, Department of Biology, for the Cynipid Wasp (on p. 58), from his private collection, by permission.
- Richard Leung, for the Thrips (on p. 60), Cheryl Moorehead for the Sawfly (on p. 59), Lynette Schimming, for the Rose Curculio (on p. 55), and Steve Scott, for the Leafcutter Bee (on p. 57), and Rose Slug (on p. 59), all images used by permission and found at <**http://bugguide.net/node/view/15740**>.
- Susannah Anderson, for the Spittlebugs (on p. 60) used by permission and found at <**http://wanderinweeta.blogspot.com/2008/06/frogs-snakes-cuckoos-or-bugs. html**>.
- Shauneen O'Brien for the White-tailed Jackrabbit and House Mouse (both on p. 61), Brent Johner for the Meadow Vole (on p. 61), and Jim Slobodian, for the Mule Deer (on p. 61), all images used by permission and found at Talk About Wildlife, the Weaselhead Society News blog at <**http://talkaboutwildlife.ca/profile/id.php**>.

❀ ❀ ❀